T0323193

THE COMET
ESCAPE LINE

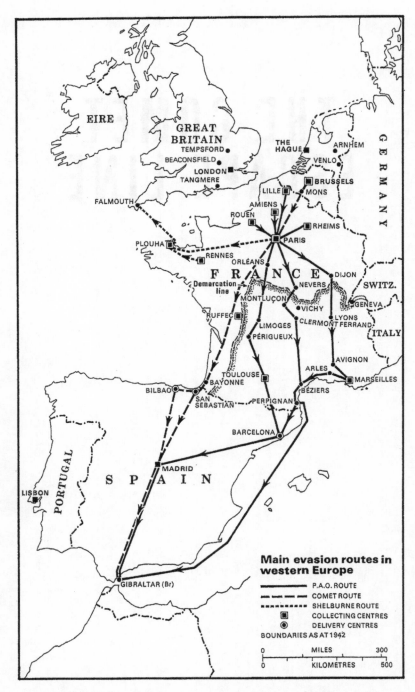

Main evasion routes in Western Europe from *MI9 Escape and Evasion 1939–1945*
by Michael Foot and J.M. Langley. (Reprinted by permission of Peters Fraser &
Dunlop (www.petersfraserdunlop.com) on behalf of the estate of Michael Foot)

THE COMET ESCAPE LINE

The Inside Story of the Most Successful Escape Line of the Second World War

ALEXANDER STILWELL

The History Press

First published 2024

The History Press
97 St George's Place, Cheltenham,
Gloucestershire, GL50 3QB
www.thehistorypress.co.uk

British Library Cataloguing in Publication Data.
A catalogue record for this book is available from the British Library.

ISBN 978 0 7509 9743 0

Typesetting and origination by The History Press
Printed and bound in Great Britain by TJ Books Limited, Padstow, Cornwall

Trees for Life

Contents

Introduction

The Gestapo officer looked across his desk at the young woman. He had a file on his desk that had told him something about her, including the previous occasions that she had been interrogated since her arrest, but it did not tell him very much. Her expression was implacable, emphasised by youthful skin drawn tight over high cheekbones, hair swept back from a strong brow and a feminine mouth that was firmly closed. Most impressive were her eyes, which were scintillatingly clear and showed no fear, even though she must be well aware of what the Gestapo were capable of doing in order to extract the information that they needed.

What did they know? That she was a significant player in an escape line that had taken up so many intelligence and police resources to track down. They had received a useful tip-off from a collaborator more interested in money than loyalty. But now they had her it just did not seem to make sense. She looked so young. Surely it was impossible that this young woman – little more than a schoolgirl – could be the head of an organisation that was helping hundreds of Allied servicemen travel the length of France to the Spanish border and freedom. They had run rings around the Geheime Staatspolizei, known as the Gestapo, the Geheime Feldpolizei, or Wehrmacht secret military police, and the Abwehr, or German military intelligence for the Reichswehr and Wehrmacht. The interrogator regarded himself as a good judge of character and he knew how to spot weaknesses. Torture was so unsubtle for a man of his intelligence and so unsuitable for a young woman like this, but he decided to play with the idea anyway. The face remained impassive.

What made it even more difficult was that this young woman had already told them that she was the leader of the escape line.[1] How could that be true? Surely an operation that had caused the personal intervention of Reichsmarschall Hermann Göring could not be run by a schoolgirl? How can you continue to interrogate someone who has already given you an answer that you are not prepared to believe?

The young woman waited. She was clearly tired and hungry, exhausted both from the long hours of interrogation and from fear and the deprivations of a crowded cell, shared with other women in various stages of despair.

The interrogator looked back at his open dossier. He was an intelligent man. Intelligent enough to know when he was beaten. He closed the dossier and left the room.

This was January 1943, and the young woman was Andrée de Jongh. The story of how she came to be of such interest to the Nazi Gestapo begins about thirty years earlier.

German Invasion of Belgium in the First World War

The long-standing rivalry between Germany and France before 1914 put Belgium in a perilous position. Armies had fought across Belgium before. Generals such as Marlborough, Wellington and Napoleon had found glory or met their Waterloo. Now tensions in Europe were reaching breaking point. Germany was planning to unleash its Schlieffen Plan,[2] which would wrong-foot formidable French defences by sending an advance through Belgium and running a ring behind French defences while drawing the French defences at the front towards the east and into the jaws of a trap. To achieve this, Belgium itself would need to be invaded, despite its neutrality. As the German armies advanced in August 1914 and overcame the formidable Belgian fortresses at Liège, the main Belgian Army moved to positions in Flanders while the Belgian Government moved to Le Havre. More than 90 per cent of Belgium was occupied by the Germans. Belgium had a defensive alliance with

Great Britain and, technically, the violation of Belgium's neutrality brought Great Britain into the First World War. In the Battle of the Frontiers, large German and French forces fought across the French and Belgian borders. After a series of German victories, the German advance was finally brought to a halt with the aid of the British Expeditionary Force (BEF) at the Marne. With a French thrust towards Lorraine, the German commander Moltke[3] was tempted to try for a quick victory and the Schlieffen Plan began to unravel. At the First Battle of the Marne (5–12 September 1914), French and British forces had regained their composure and successfully counter-attacked the Germans. At the First Battle of Ypres and the Yser (19 October–30 November 1914), the Belgian Army lost about 20,000 men while the Germans lost 130,000. By the end of 1914, armies on both sides had settled down into trench warfare and an ensuing defensive war of attrition.

The majority of Belgium was now under German military rule and any Belgian resistance in occupied areas was strictly punished. Caught in the middle of the invasion was an English nurse called Edith Cavell. The daughter of an English vicar and born in Norwich, she had worked as a nurse at The London Hospital and had moved to Brussels in 1907 at the invitation of Dr Antoine Depage to be the matron of a new nursing school, L'École Belge d'Infirmières Diplomées. She was responsible for training nurses in three hospitals as well as schools, and in due course became matron of a new hospital at St-Gilles in the centre of Brussels.[4] On the outbreak of war in 1914, the hospitals came under the control of the Red Cross. Once the German military authorities had taken control of Brussels, Cavell began to take care of wounded soldiers of all nationalities from the front line and devised a plan to help them across the border to neutral Holland.

Cavell was at the centre of a network that included a wide range of Belgians, including aristocrats such as Prince Reginald de Croy and his wife Princess Marie de Croy, based at the Château de Bellignies near Mons; the Countess de Belleville, who provided shelter for men at her house in Montignies-sur-Roc; the chemist Louis Severin; and the architect Philippe Baucq. A Jesuit priest, Father Persoul, also helped evaders to reach the border.[5]

It was not long before the German authorities became suspicious and the matter became the responsibility of Lieutenant Bergan, head of espionage in the German secret police. Bergan and his associates ran a wide network of spies and informers and, however discreet Cavell and her associates might be, they could never be entirely sure that people who came to their door or who hovered outside in the street were not working for the authorities. While the number of evaders increased, the net was also tightening on the escape organisation.

Other factors made it difficult for evaders to get across the border. After a German submarine sank the Dutch ship *Catwyk* in April 1915, Holland came to the brink of war and sentries were placed at 15m intervals along the border, which was also mined.

As an increasing number of strangers with unconvincing stories came to her door and to those of her helpers, Cavell resolved to continue undeterred. A particularly effective informer for the Germans was a Frenchman called Georges Gaston Quien, who was responsible for a growing number of arrests.

In August 1915, the secret police finally struck. Cavell and one of her nurses called Sister Wilkins were arrested. They were taken to police headquarters and interrogated by Lieutenant Bergan. Wilkins was allowed to leave but Cavell was placed in the crowded women's cell in the Kommandantur in Brussels. Two others in the rescue network, the Countess de Belleville and Louise Thuliez, were also arrested. On 7 August, Cavell was moved to the prison at St-Gilles, where she was placed in solitary confinement. On 8 August she was interrogated at Police Station B by Lieutenant Bergan, assisted by the chief officer of criminal investigation, Sergeant Pinkhoff, Sergeant Neuhaus and a spy called Otto Meyer.[6]

The interrogation was confusing for Cavell who, apart from the stress of arrest and confinement, was asked questions in German that were then translated into French. She replied in French and the transcription was then made in German, making it impossible for Cavell to check its accuracy before she was asked to sign it. This allowed incriminatory nuances to be put into the text without her noticing. After the interrogation, Cavell was returned to her cell for weeks of solitary confinement while she awaited trial.

Cavell's arrest was brought to the attention of senior members of the British Government, including the Foreign Secretary Edward Grey. Grey asked the United States Ambassador in London to make inquiries through the American legation in Brussels, which was headed by Brand Whitlock. He in turn wrote to the head of the Politische Abteilung, Baron von der Lancken-Wakenitz, suggesting that the legal adviser to the American legation, Gaston Leval, might be entrusted with Cavell's defence. Receiving no reply, Whitlock repeated the request, upon which he received a reply two days later informing him that Cavell had admitted to the charges against her and that she could not be interviewed while in solitary confinement. Von der Lancken's letter included the ominous assertion that Cavell had helped men 'desirous of proceeding to the front'. This directly implied that Cavell had been involved in reinforcing Germany's enemies.[7]

To make matters worse for Cavell, the new military governor-general for Belgium was a hardliner called General von Sauberzweig. He was an advocate of any means required to quell resistance and to maintain order. A recalcitrant Englishwoman was very much a fly in his orderly ointment.

The trial was predictably one-sided, but the judges' conclusions were nonetheless shocking. Edith Cavell, Philippe Baucq, Louise Thuliez, Louis Severin and Jeaunne Belleville were all sentenced to death. Others were given sentences of up to two years' hard labour, according to the level of their involvement. When she was informed that she could appeal, Cavell replied: 'No, it is useless. I am English.' Sauberzweig confirmed her prediction and ordered that the sentence should be carried out immediately. The execution would take place at 7 a.m. the next day, 12 October 1915.

In the small window of time that was available, hurried diplomatic efforts were made by Belgian legal aid adviser Gaston de Laval, Brand Whitlock and the Spanish Minister in Brussels, the Marquis de Villalobar. In the event, their efforts proved to be fruitless. The British Foreign Office took the view that any direct intervention by them would only make matters worse.[8]

A German Lutheran pastor contacted an Anglican priest in Brussels, the Reverend Stirling Gahan. He visited Cavell in her cell that night to give her the Holy Sacrament. When he said that she would be remembered as a martyr, she replied that she was just a nurse who had tried to do her duty.

The next morning, she and Baucq were taken to the national shooting range, the Tir National, in Schaerbeek, where 250 soldiers awaited them. The open expanse had a large, grassed slope at the end to soak up the bullets. It was cold, wet and muddy. In front of the slope there were two white posts and next to them two coffins. Two groups of eight soldiers were formed up in front of each post. Cavell and Baucq were bound to the posts and then blindfolded. Cavell spoke to the Lutheran pastor in attendance: '*Ma conscience est tranquille. Je meurs pour Dieu et ma patrie.*' Meanwhile, the firing squad were informed by a German officer that they should have no qualms due to the horrendous crimes that the man and woman before them had committed.[9]

The doctor in attendance commented: 'She went to her death with a bearing which is quite impossible to forget.'

He went on: 'There is a fear lest her death should lead to disorders. … We must hurry and silence and secrecy should surround her grave.'[10]

Some hope. A legend had been created.

The bullets that caused Cavell to slump forward against her restraints had a similar effect to the German U-boat torpedoes that penetrated the hull of the British liner *Lusitania* on 7 May 1915, near the southern coast of Ireland, as it crossed the Atlantic from New York. Both events sent shockwaves around the world. Far from ridding themselves of an exasperating Englishwoman who represented all that they loved to hate about England, the German authorities handed their enemies a propaganda coup.

The murder of a nurse was seen as proof of German villainy and protests were made at the highest levels, including by King Alphonso XIII of Spain and President Woodrow Wilson. The German Kaiser, seeing which way the wind was blowing, ordered that there should be no further executions of women without his express permission. He also rescinded the death sentences that had been given to the other plaintiffs in the case.

Recruitment in Britain rose exponentially as young men rallied to the call to avenge the death of Edith Cavell. Monuments began to be erected, including one in St Martin's Place in London, while Queen

Alexandra ordered that a nurse's home at The London Hospital that had been intended to carry her name should instead be named after Cavell. Her chaplain wrote to Edith's mother:

> I am commanded by Her Majesty Queen Alexandra to write and say how deeply Her Majesty feels for you in the sad and tragic loss of your daughter ... always remember that she never failed England in her time of need ... The name of Miss Cavell will be held in highest honour and respect ...[11]

By 1918, five Cavell homes had been created. King Albert of Belgium posthumously awarded Cavell the Cross of the Order of Leopold, the Belgian Government awarded her the Croix Civique and France awarded her the Légion d'honneur.

When the war ended, Edith Cavell's body, which had been placed in what the German authorities hoped would be an unremembered grave, was carried in a gun carriage through the streets of Brussels and then by train to Ostend, where a Royal Navy battleship HMS *Rowena* was waiting to carry it across the Channel to Dover. Here a train took it to Victoria Station, where a gun carriage carried the coffin in procession to Westminster Abbey escorted by 100 soldiers and accompanied by a band. After a service at the Abbey, the coffin was then taken to Liverpool Street Station for the journey to Norwich, where a burial service took place before the coffin was interred in the Cathedral grounds.

However, there was another way in which Cavell's witness was remembered. It was taken into the hearts of the Belgian people, with whom she had worked in solidarity during their oppression. Cavell in turn had shown personal admiration for the people among whom she had worked as a nurse for so long. In a letter to her mother, she had written: 'What do you think of these people: they have suffered and are suffering a martyrdom and in silence. Their attitude is wonderful in reserve and in dignity.'[12]

Belgium had not just been held in check while the Germans had got on with the war in the trenches; parts of the country had been devastated, as witnessed by the Catholic Cardinal Mercier in his pastoral letter of Christmas 1914: Patriotism and Endurance:

At Louvain, a third of the town has been destroyed and 1074 buildings have disappeared. ... Thousands of Belgian citizens have been
deported to German prisons – to Munster, to Celle, to Magdeburg.
Munster alone has 3,100 civilian prisoners ... Thousands have
been shot. ... In my diocese alone, I know thirteen priests have
been executed.[13]

The priceless library of the University of Leuven had also been
burned to the ground.

Edith Cavell saw it as a natural duty not only to help British,
French and Belgian servicemen but to be part of the resistance within
a neutral nation allied to her own country that had been unlawfully
occupied. In this respect, her duty to escaping servicemen was as
clear as her duty to her patients. The hospital provided a convenient
cover for some of her activities, where evaders were disguised as
wounded. It is also worth noting that, apart from her nursing staff,
some of whom were English, many helpers in the evasion lines were
Belgian women, including aristocrats such as Baronesses de Croy and
Belleville and other ordinary people such as a widow who provided
shelter and food for the men whom Cavell passed on to her.

It would be possible to go into much more detail about Cavell's
activities and those of her Belgian resistance helpers but suffice it to
say that history would repeat itself.

In November 1916, a girl named Andrée was born to Paul and
Alice de Jongh in the north-eastern district of Schaerbeek, where
Cavell had died almost exactly a year previously, and she was des-
tined to play a major role in the next war.

After a series of massive strikes on the Western Front in 1918,
the German armies under General Ludendorff had shot their bolt.
Despite causing huge casualties to the Allies, their bulges into the
Allied lines invited counter-attacks from French, British, Australian
and Canadian forces, increasingly bolstered by reinforcements
from the United States. The Allied counter-attacks, often supported by tanks, left German forces with little to fall back on and by
8 August 1918 at the Battle of Amiens Ludendorff acknowledged
that the game was up. He advised Kaiser William II that negotiations for peace should be pursued to avoid a catastrophe. Meanwhile,

continued Allied offensives pushed German forces back behind the Hindenburg Line, their start point at the beginning of the year.

Another concerted Allied offensive was planned for September that included an advance by the Belgian Army from Ypres towards Ghent. However, the Allies failed to achieve all their objectives, giving renewed hope to some German military commanders that they would not be militarily defeated after all. However, Ludendorff's scepticism soon spread throughout Germany and public opinion largely turned against the continuation of the war. The German Grand Fleet mutinied when ordered to set out from Kiel for a final showdown with the Royal Navy and there was now a spirit of revolution as communists and others took advantage of the discontent. President Wilson of the United States sent a note to Germany saying that he would recommend an armistice if Germany agreed to render itself incapable of further hostilities. On 8 November representatives of the two warring sides met in the forest of Compiègne northeast of Paris. Here the Germans learned that the Allies were seeking substantial war reparations. Kaiser William II abdicated and a socialdemocrat, Friedrich Ebert, became Chancellor. The Armistice was signed on 11 November 1918 at 11 a.m. and the war came to an end.

German forces had by then retreated, using a scorched earth policy to slow the Allied advance. Although the prospects looked grim for the Germans, they still had substantial forces in being. The German delegation at Compiègne was led by a civilian and this planted the seed of an idea that Germany had been betrayed while she was still militarily capable of continuing the fight. The sense was further fomented by the massive scale of concessions and reparations that Germany was required to make. In due course, one of the most prominent exponents of this idea of betrayal of German arms would be a corporal who had served in the trenches by the name of Adolf Hitler.

During the course of the war, the Belgian King Albert had remained in command of Belgian troops and was a frequent visitor to the trenches from his headquarters at De Panne, a few miles along the coast north-east of Dunkirk.

As Belgium got on with rebuilding from the wreckage of the Great War under the leadership of King Albert I, Germany formed a new republic at Weimar in August 1919. Although things seemed

to be on a democratic footing for Germany, there was bitter-
ness throughout Germany at the terms imposed by the Treaty of
Versailles. Germany lost just under 90,000 square miles of territory
and control over 7 million people. Reparations paid to the Allies
were in the order of 20 billion marks to begin with. Military hard-
ware was limited and military aircraft were forbidden altogether.
The responsibility for the war was officially placed on Germany's
shoulders. The alternative to signing was invasion by the Allies. The
treaty was signed on 28 June 1919. The Weimar Republic then proceeded with a doubly poisoned chalice, having betrayed a supposedly
undefeated German army and given in to crushing treaty terms. In
due course, resentment led to the formation of parties such as the
German Racial Freedom Party and the National Socialists under
Hitler, based in Munich.

Through the 1920s, there was rampant inflation in Germany and
temporary occupation of the Ruhr by French and German troops.
In 1925, Field Marshal Paul von Hindenburg succeeded Ebert as
President. In the Pact of Locarno, Germany pledged not to inter-
fere with the borders of either Belgium or France. The treaty was
underwritten by Great Britain. The German economy began to pick
up towards the end of the 1920s but the issue of substantial war
reparations remained. The Nationalists and Nazis demanded that the
Government should refuse to pay. By 1929, the Great Depression
had struck, giving more fuel to the discontent of the Nazis and
Nationalists. Hitler spelled it out at a rally in Munich: 'We are the
result of the distress for which others are responsible.'

On 30 January 1933, Hitler became Chancellor. The next year
he declared himself Führer, or supreme leader. On 12 March 1938,
German forces entered Austria under the so-called Anschluss,
though no formal request had been made for the invasion. Hitler
then turned his attention to Czechoslovakia, where he managed to
get behind the formidable Czech defences by claiming that he had
been invited to take over the Sudetenland. This happened with both
French and British connivance as they cravenly conceded to Hitler's
demands in the naive hope that he would not want more. Poland was
bound by treaty with Britain and France and when German forces
crossed the Polish border on 1 September 1939 there were no further

options. The British Empire and France declared war on Germany on 3 September 1939 and the Second World War began.

Operation Fall Gelb

The new German plan for the invasion of the Low Countries and France involved two main armies, Army Group A and Army Group B. Army Group A would attack through southern Belgium and then make a move to the north in order to allow in more Allied reserves. Army Group B, meanwhile, would attack through the Ardennes in the south in a surprise thrust against reserve French forces. The plan incorporated the radical ideas of Heinz Guderian,[14] who planned to make a radical thrust with his Panzers from the Ardennes up towards the Channel.

However, there were formidable defences and obstacles to be overcome on the Dutch and Belgian borders for which the Germans had devised sophisticated plans. One was the formidable fortress of Ében-Émael. Considered impregnable, it was attacked by elements of the 7th Airborne Division (Student) of the Luftwaffe and the 22nd Infantry Division, an army airborne battalion, mainly embarked on gliders. The units were supported by Luftflotte II under Albert Kesselring. Fort Ében-Émael was armed with two 120mm guns and sixteen 75mm guns in armoured turrets and casemates. It held the right flank of the Belgian line on the Albert Canal. The German glider detachment consisted of forty-two gliders formed under Captain Walter Koch, comprising 424 men, including the pilots. The advantage provided by gliders was that they were totally silent on approach, whereas planes dropping parachutists would have attracted attention. Some German gliders landed among the defences covering the bridges of the Veldweezelt and Vroenhoven. Koch's men then cut the demolition charge wires to the bridges as well as telephone wires. The other eleven gliders landed directly on top of Fort Ében-Émael. Assault engineers attached explosive charges to the turrets and casemates with about 2½ tons of explosives. After the fort had been neutralised, German reinforcements of the 4th Division soon began to move up, followed by the XVI Panzer Corps and the 6th Army.

Once Fort Ében-Émael had surrendered, the Belgian 7th Division was ordered to withdraw. King Leopold of Belgium sent his troops a reassuring if optimistic message:

> Our position improves day by day; our ranks are tightening. In the decisive days which lie ahead do not spare yourselves; suffer every sacrifice to halt the invasion. As on the Yser in 1914, the French and British Corps are relying on us; the safety and honour of the country demands it.[15]

By 15 May, the French 1st Army, deployed between Namur and Wavre, was under attack by the German 6th Army, supported by Stuka dive bombers. The German XI Corps attacked Louvain but was successfully counter-attacked by the British 3rd Division under General Bernard Montgomery.

Further to the south, German forces had even greater success. The thinly spread French forces lacked both anti-aircraft and anti-tank guns, which put them at a huge disadvantage when dealing with Stukas and German armour. Major General Erwin Rommel reached Houx on the Meuse and established a small bridgehead that French forces failed to counter-attack effectively. General Heinz Guderian's XIX Panzer Corps reached Sedan. Panzergruppe Kleist and XIV Panzer Corps blew a breach through the French 1st Army and more than 2,000 German Panzers began to race towards the Channel. Attempts by French forces to mount a counter-attack were hampered by German bomber attacks on the railway system, effectively sealing off the German area of operations, and by roads filled with panicking refugees.

Fortunately for the Allies, someone else was beginning to panic. His name was Adolf Hitler. With the success of the advance beyond the wildest dreams of German high command, Hitler became concerned that the Panzers might overreach themselves and get bogged down in the softer ground near the Channel coast. On 24 May, therefore, he gave his famous halt order, stopping the Panzers at a line running through Lens, Bethune, St-Omer and Gravelines.

Having surrendered Brussels and Antwerp on 17 May, the Belgian Army continued to hold along a line from the Leopold Canal to the Lys canal where it joined the left flank of the British Expeditionary

Force (BEF) at Menin. On 24 May, the German 6th Army broke through at Courtrai, upon which it was counter-attacked by the Belgian 8th Division and 2nd Chasseurs Ardennais. On 25 May the Belgian 12th Division also counter-attacked but found itself short of reserves. British forces, meanwhile, continued to withdraw towards Dunkirk. By 26 May the Belgian Army was under attack on two fronts – it was threatened on its right flank by the German Reichenau Division and on its left by the German 18th Army coming from the direction of Antwerp.

King Leopold realised that Belgian forces could not hold out much longer but, while he sent an envoy to the Germans to discuss surrender terms, he also arranged for the shipment of the French 60th Division to Dunkirk and the blocking of the ports of Ostend and Zeebrugge, along with the destruction of the bridges over the Yser. By 28 May the Belgian Army had ceased fire.

Unlike Queen Wilhelmina of the Netherlands, who had escaped to England along with the Dutch Government, as commander-in-chief of Belgian forces Leopold chose to remain with his troops. The Belgian Government, however, decamped to London. The continued resistance of the Belgian Army, holding German forces to the east of Dunkirk, had bought valuable time for British, French and Belgian troops to evacuate from Dunkirk. To the south of Dunkirk, French forces of the 1st Army continued to put up a fight, although they were eventually overwhelmed.

On 29 May, more than 47,000 troops were embarked from Dunkirk. These were transported on 850 commercial boats that had been taken over by the British Admiralty along with the thirty-nine destroyers and escorts used in the operation. The boats embarked troops from Dunkirk itself, Malo-les-Bains, Bray-Dunes and De Panne.

On 30 May, 120,000 troops, including 6,000 French soldiers, were embarked for England. On 31 May, this figure rose to 150,000, including about 15,000 French. By 4 June, 113,000 French and Belgian troops had been shipped to England, and on the last four days of the operation 75,000 British and 98,000 French troops were embarked. In total, 198,000 British and 140,000 French and Belgian troops were saved.

The evacuation craft and ships were attacked by German E-boats and by Stukas, which sank about a quarter of the small craft as well as seven French and six British destroyers. RAF Bomber Command, Fighter Command and Coastal Command flew 2,739 sorties and 651 bombing raids as well as 177 reconnaissance flights. They shot down 262 German aircraft with a loss of 106 of their own.

Not everyone got away, of course. Some units were separated, and some men did not get to the beaches on time. The 51st (Highland) Division, for example, was not part of the BEF that advanced into Belgium. The 51st was instead attached to the French 10th Army and was drawn back to form a defensive line along the Somme, following a line from north-west of Abbeville to the coast. Under sustained German attack, the division withdrew to the river Bresle. After German attacks cut off supply lines, the 51st fell back to Bethune.

As the situation deteriorated, a decision was made to retreat to Le Havre for evacuation and an advance unit called Ark Force was despatched to hold the port, pending the arrival of the rest of the division. However, it soon became clear that the speed of the German advance would make it difficult for the rest of the division to reach Le Havre, let alone embark for England. General Fortune therefore decided to move the division to St-Valery-en-Caux.

By the time they reached St-Valery, under continuous pressure from the Germans, they were short of food and ammunition. Advancing German forces were supported by tanks and the 51st had no anti-tank guns. Its remaining 25pdr guns had been put out of action. On 12 June both the French Chasseurs Alpins and the 51st Highland Division surrendered to avoid further casualties.

Although the Navy had approached St-Valery on 10 June, due to fog and German artillery on the cliffs, it had withdrawn. For the same reasons, evacuation was all but impossible. The Admiralty had despatched sixty-seven merchant ships and 140 small vessels to the St-Valery area. However, there were difficulties in communications and little knowledge among the flotilla about the time and the place for embarkation. When boats were despatched to St-Valery, they came under enemy fire and air attack and withdrew. They then encountered fog, making it even more difficult to communicate with those inland.

A naval officer reported:

I do not, however, consider that any great number would in any case have been evacuated from St-Valery area. On 10th June enemy batteries fired on our ships. By 9.30 on 11th June, the enemy were machine-gunning our ships off St-Valery, and by noon enemy had guns in position on coast to dominate beaches and later on to dominate that part of the town in which our troops were crowded.[16]

There were some successful efforts by small craft to take men off, however, even under enemy fire. Men were taken off the beaches at Veules-les-Roses and one boat managed to take off eighty men at St-Valery.

Ark Force, having reached Le Havre on 10 June, had been safely embarked. It would form the kernel of the revived 51st that would continue to see action throughout the war, including in North Africa.

Two destroyers despatched from the Le Havre area to St-Valery were HMS *Bulldog* and HMS *Boadicea*. On 10 June, the *Boadicea* picked up sixty soldiers of the 51st and some French civilians. The *Bulldog* also picked up a boat full of soldiers from further out to sea. The destroyers came under fire from German artillery and tanks on the cliffs above St-Valery but the destroyers fired back with their main armament and silenced the enemy. However, the two destroyers then came under aerial attack from Stukas.

The *Boadicea* was attacked by eighteen Ju 87 Stukas and sustained three direct hits, which caused many casualties. The *Boadicea*'s engines were put out of action, but the destroyer *Ambuscade* approached to take her in tow. The *Bulldog* was attacked by six Stukas but was less severely damaged and suffered only minor casualties. Although the two destroyers were effectively sitting ducks for a renewed aerial attack, despite the hot June weather a thick fog descended over the ships, sheltering them for the rest of the afternoon and that night. The *Boadicea* was towed back to Portsmouth by the *Ambuscade*, while the *Bulldog* managed to get back to the Isle of Wight under limited power. However, the same fog that had protected the two destroyers from almost certain obliteration also prevented any further attempts to embark more troops.

Captain B.C. Bradford was among those captured and marched east as prisoners of war (PoWs) after the surrender of the 51st (Highland) Division at St-Valery. The weather was extremely hot and the PoWs were given very little food or water by their captors. The Highlanders were already exhausted enough from their fighting retreat to St-Valery and to this was added the fatigue of despondency after being captured. Occasionally the prisoners would break into a local house to get some much-needed water, cider or red wine.[17]

After long marches and nights in filthy farmyards, Bradford eventually managed to step out of the column and get off the road unnoticed by the German guards. He then made his way to a wood, where he lay down on the swampy ground with his mackintosh over his head to keep off the mosquitoes. When the column had moved on, he managed to get a local to bring him some civilian clothes and then made his way to Boulogne, staying at farms along the way. However, his hopes of finding a boat to take him across the Channel were dashed and the only alternative seemed to be to head south in the hope of reaching Spain.

As he made his way south, Bradford stayed in barns and received hospitality from several locals. Although there were plenty of Germans around, at this stage of the war they were still on the move and a more elaborate system of checks had not yet been established. The Germans were aware that local populations had been displaced by the invasion and that it was not unusual or surprising for civilians to be found outside their locality or without papers. The fact that Bradford did not possess any papers was therefore less of a problem than it might have been.

Having swum across the river Cher that runs across central France, Bradford soon came upon French soldiers, who insisted that he should stay with them. This was an uncomfortable experience for Bradford due to the tensions that existed after the retreat where French troops had sometimes been forcibly prevented from boarding British vessels at Dunkirk as well as at St-Valery. Moving on to Toulouse, he was put in touch with a guide who would provide him with directions over the Pyrenees. After a difficult climb during which they encountered some snow, the pair crossed the Spanish border at Port de Baroude, south-west of Lourdes in the central Pyrenees. They then descended to the Cirque de Barrosa. When they reached a track at the bottom of a steep incline, they heard a shout behind them. The Guardia Civil told them to get back over the border on Franco's orders. When they protested, they were taken to see a local mayor, who happened to be an anti-British Falangist.

Having been pushed back over the frontier, Bradford managed to find another guide who was prepared to help him over the mountains for money. He was arrested again by the Spanish authorities and taken to a concentration camp at Monferran-Savès. After whatever diplomatic alchemy had taken place, he eventually found his way to Algiers and from there to Gibraltar.[18]

Bradford was not, of course, the only one to have been left behind after the Dunkirk evacuations. Including the 51st (Highland) Division, 68,000 soldiers were not evacuated, including the hospitalised, wounded and those who died. Many soldiers tried to make their way home independently, either before capture by the Germans or after escaping from captivity during the long marches towards the PoW camps in Germany.

British troops of the BEF who had advanced into Belgium ran into the retreating Belgian Army and soon found themselves beating a hasty retreat. They had had little time to establish strong defensive positions in Belgium like the ones that had been built in France. The retreating soldiers were mixed up with large columns of civilian evacuees and the columns were attacked regularly by German aircraft.

Between 16 and 19 May, the withdrawal had moved rapidly from the Dyle Line to the Escaut Line, with somewhat desperate rearguard actions being fought to give the engineers time to demolish bridges. The Sussex Regiment, West Kent Regiment and The Buffs (Royal East Kent Regiment) were systematically bombed and shelled at Mont des Cats before continuing their retreat towards Dunkirk. In these engagements men became separated from their units, some were captured and some managed to evade.

The temporary setback suffered by the advancing Panzers at Arras and the halt order given by Hitler played alongside British and French efforts to reinforce and defend the Channel ports, mainly Calais, Boulogne and Dunkirk. On 21 and 22 May, British reinforcements under Brigadier Nicholson in the form of 30th Infantry Brigade (2nd King's Royal Rifle Corps, 1st Rifle Brigade and 1st Queen Victoria's Rifles, supplemented by 3rd Tank Regiment and 29th Anti-Tank Battery) arrived in Calais. Queen Victoria's Rifles were deployed into the surrounding countryside to block the approaches to the town. Their mission had been set out rather starkly by the Rt Hon. Sir Anthony Eden, Secretary of State for War: 'Defence of Calais to utmost is of vital importance to our country and BEF and as showing our continued co-operation with France.'[19]

There was plenty of cause for concern for the British garrison at Calais in these words, which continue to be at the centre of a controversy over whether the defence of Calais 'to the utmost' or the need to show 'co-operation with France' was necessary. Whether at Calais or anywhere else, defensive efforts only had a realistic hope of slowing the inevitable German advance rather than stopping it in its tracks. Calais came to be seen as a political pawn to be played off against the French, if not a lamb for sacrifice. What is not in doubt is that British and French forces did indeed defend the port town to the utmost. As the German 1st Panzer Division approached from the south, outlying forces beat a fighting retreat into the centre of the town, where Nicholson realised he would have to concentrate his defence. The garrison, mostly centred on the citadel, endured German shelling and ground attacks as well as aerial bombing by Stukas for four days. By Sunday 26 May, the Germans were beginning to occupy the north of the town while groups of British riflemen put up a stiff defence street by street to slow their advance. By 3 p.m., however, the garrison had been overwhelmed.

Although a handful of British troops had been taken off a jetty by a British yacht, Brigadier Nicholson had been forbidden from embarking his brigade and the chance of saving hundreds of British troops from death or imprisonment.

Fortunately for the defenders of Boulogne, the same did not apply to them. By 22 May, Boulogne had been reinforced by 20th Guards Brigade (Welsh and Irish Guards) under Brigadier William Fox-Pitt. The port was also defended by French and Belgian soldiers. The

Guards had enough time to dig defensive positions before the German 2nd Panzer Corps attacked. By 23 May, the outlying defences had been pushed back into the town while about eighty RAF light bombers of the Advanced Air Striking Force provided support as British and French destroyers bombarded German positions. On 23 May the Guards brigade was ordered to embark and Royal Navy destroyers, including HMS *Venomous* and HMS *Windsor*, braved the fire of German artillery as they entered the port, which had already been damaged by the Luftwaffe. Not all the British troops made it to the port in time for the embarkation. The 3rd Company, Welsh Guards, under Major Windsor-Lewis had been cut off from the rest of the battalion. Windsor-Lewis organised a sterling defence of the Gare Maritime, but eventually they were overwhelmed and forced to surrender.

Although hundreds were taken prisoner after the siege of Calais, some, like Private Gordon Instone of the 1st Searchlight Regiment, Royal Artillery, managed to escape. Instone had been pulled back with the rest of his unit as news was received of the fall of Boulogne and the approach of German forces from the south. In the hope that at least some of the Calais garrison might be embarked, Instone and others were marched to the harbour to wait for a ship. However, all too soon there was a counter-order and they were all marched back into the town with orders to fight to the end. As the situation continued to deteriorate, it was only a matter of time before they were either killed or captured. Instone and others desperately sought refuge on the beach, which of course provided no cover. They could just see England, tantalisingly visible across the sea. Those who did not succumb to German machine guns were eventually rounded up and taken prisoner. Instone joined a column of PoWs but soon tried to escape by diving under a hedge. He was seen by the German guards and told that he would be shot if he tried to escape again. However, while the column was passing through St-Pol, he saw his opportunity and jumped into a stream. He hid among the reeds until the Germans had given up searching for him and the column had moved on. He managed to find a barn where he could hide, dry out and try to recover some energy. Instone and the rest of the Calais garrison had barely had any sleep during the siege and little food. Muddled by exhaustion, he was unclear about where to head next. Belgium and Holland were both occupied, and Switzerland seemed very remote, even if he managed to evade the Germans in order to get there. At this relatively early stage of the war there was still a reasonable possibility for evaders to get away from the Channel coast but the chances of doing so were diminishing by the day as the Wehrmacht, Luftwaffe and Kriegsmarine took control.[20]

Instone left his farm refuge and continued on this way, eating whatever vegetables he could find in fields, until he came across a friendly farmer who provided him with shelter, food and civilian clothing. Later, he was sheltered in a centre for the aged and met another British evader, Flight Lieutenant Wilfred Treacy. Treacy had already tried to escape by boat. The first time, when searching for a boat with some soldiers of the Black Watch, he had been spotted by German soldiers and taken for questioning. Sent to a concentration camp, he managed to escape and headed back to the coast. He found a boat on a river inlet near the Baie d'Authie. However, having been delayed by low tide, it was morning before he could row out to sea. He was soon spotted by a machine gun post on the cliffs, which opened fire on him. Treacy kept going until he was out of range. Around midday a German aircraft flying from Le Touquet signalled to him to turn round and when he did not it opened fire on him before flying off. Later a German seaplane landed near him and it was all over for his escape attempt. He was taken back to prison and interrogated by the Luftwaffe at Boulogne. After being moved from one location to another, Treacy managed to escape again and found refuge with a friendly farmer near Bouveries.[21]

Meanwhile, Instone had been arrested by a German officer and was put on the back of a truck to be sent to a labour camp. He managed to overcome both his guards and jumped off the truck when it slowed at a corner. Falling in with a French officer, he made his way to Paris, where he stayed with the Frenchman's family. Having acquired forged papers, he made his way over the demarcation line, only to be arrested on the other side. He then managed to get away and returned to cross the line again.[22]

Entering Vichy France in 1940 was by no means a ticket to freedom. Hundreds of refugees from the battles in the north, including

British, French and Belgian servicemen and many civilians, wanted to get to ports such as Marseilles in the hope of escaping by sea. The Armistice agreement between the Vichy Government and Germany included a clause that the Vichy Government would prevent servicemen from returning to England or any other country for that matter. On 14 July 1940, the Vichy Government gave an order that all British servicemen should be detained at Fort St-Jean in Marseilles harbour. Initially, the arrangements were fairly relaxed, with British servicemen being allowed to go into the city on parole. However, after a German commission paid a visit, arrangements became more strict.

Both Instone and Treacy learned of a plan to transfer the prisoners at Fort St-Jean to a concentration camp at St Hippolyte near Nimes in January and they resolved to make an attempt to cross the Pyrenees in December. The plan was to take a train to Perpignan at the eastern end of the Pyrenees where the hills were relatively low and then find their way over the border before heading for the British consulate in Barcelona. Instone made his escape attempt with several others, crossing the Pyrenees with a French guide. However, the guide soon lost his way. They made for Figueras in the hope of catching a train for Barcelona but they were arrested by Spanish Guardias Civiles and taken to Cervera, where they were confined in a small cell. They were then moved via Zaragoza jail to the concentration camp at Miranda de Ebro, about 50 miles south of Bilbao, where they stayed for four months in appalling conditions. Instone and others were released in March 1941 and reached Gibraltar later that month.

Meanwhile, like other British servicemen, Treacy had been detained and taken to Fort St-Jean, where he was appointed officer in charge of escapes. His deputy was Lieutenant Colonel Jimmy Langley, who had lost an arm at Dunkirk and whom we shall hear more of later. Treacy managed to pass himself off as an Irishman, having arranged all the necessary forged papers, including exit visas for Spain and Portugal. By 30 January 1941 he was on a plane back to England from Lisbon.[23] Having been declared unfit for military duties, Langley was repatriated in February 1941.

Although these escapes proved to be ultimately successful, it is worth noting that they took place in the early stages of the German occupation when German control had not yet been fully established and while there was still considerable movement as German forces completed the occupation and as displaced people settled down again. The escapes were also full of incident and hazards. Evaders were often arrested several times and narrowly escaped losing their lives. Some were sent to camps, where they endured poor conditions, interrogation and mistreatment. The purpose of the escape lines was to try to minimise these harrowing experiences and make the evasion journey as straightforward as possible.

The Allied Air Campaign Over Northern Europe

As the trail of evaders from the battles of the north began to dry up, the proportion of evaders involved in the air campaign continued to grow.

Initially, the pilot evaders were those who had survived being shot down, either while protecting the embarkation of troops from the beaches or carrying out tactical bombing missions against German armour or bridges as Allied forces retreated in the face of the advancing Germans. The Battle of France was followed by the Battle of Britain, largely fought over British skies, though RAF bombers attacked barges that were being assembled for the proposed invasion of England as well as German oil facilities.

In the first months of the war, British bomber aircraft were less active than they would become, and had limited navigational equipment and low-standard bombs. Their ability to even hit a large target was seriously in doubt. Working on the basis of an agreement made with the Roosevelt Government in 1939, Britain did not target civilian areas, although this would change after the Luftwaffe bombed Rotterdam in May 1940, after which the British argued that they had a right to bomb civilian areas in retaliation. The tit for tat continued after German bombers unintentionally released their bomb loads over London, having lost their way. The British retaliated by bombing Berlin, after which an enraged Hitler ordered the Luftwaffe to bomb London and other British cities, marking the beginning of the Blitz.

As the war continued into 1942, medium bombers such as the Handley Page Hampden, Armstrong Whitworth Whitley and Vickers Wellington and the large four-engine Short Stirling began to be replaced by more advanced aircraft such as the Handley Page Halifax and the Avro Lancaster. The venerable and robust Vickers Wellington medium bomber continued to carry out second-line duties. While Britain was still on the back foot, bombing provided the only means of directly striking back at the enemy and the operations, mainly carried out at night by RAF Bomber Command, became ever more intense.

In response, Germany had to invest in anti-aircraft defences while also deploying squadrons of night fighters. These were mostly twin-engine Messerschmitt Bf 110s or Junkers Ju 88s. The formidable Ju 88C was fitted with airborne intercept radar so that it could more easily intercept bombers at night, as well as two forward-firing fixed 20mm cannon.

The attrition rate for bombers was very high. It was said that you would have had a better chance of survival as an infantry officer in the Battle of the Somme than you would as a Bomber Command crew member. Of those who bailed out or escaped from a crashed bomber or occasional forced landing, 9,838 were made PoWs. Many of these attempted escapes, sometimes successful, from PoW camps such as Stalag Luft III in Lower Silesia. Out of 100 airmen, two were likely to be shot down and evade capture, their chances greatly increased if they were helped by an organised escape network.

UNITED STATES ARMY AIR FORCE

In due course, the United States Government took the view that strategic bombing was the only way to take the war to Germany, before military land operations were organised, such as the invasion of North Africa. The US Army Air Force (USAAF) deployed VIII Bomber Command to England in June 1942, and it flew its first mission over occupied Europe on 4 July 1942 with Douglas A-20 Havoc medium bombers, which were named Bostons by the RAF. One of the squadron commanders performed a hair-raising feat of flying after his aircraft was hit by flak in both wings, managing to keep his aircraft airborne and returning to base even after bouncing off the ground after the initial loss of altitude. From August, Boeing B-17 heavy bombers were deployed on missions against marshalling yards in France. USAAF target priorities developed over time with a priority list of U-boat facilities, transportation, electricity production and petroleum and rubber industries.

EARLY RAF EVADERS: THE BATTLE OF FRANCE

As the RAF squadrons based in France dealt as best they could with the Luftwaffe, the experiences of Flight Lieutenant Hedley 'Bill' Fowler were typical.[24] On 15 May, Fowler and the rest of his fellow Hurricane fighter pilots were ordered to provide cover for bombers attacking the bridges over the river Meuse. While keeping an eye on the bomber formation below him from his position at the rear of the fighter escort, Fowler saw a Messerschmitt Bf 109 making a classic attack from the sun. As he warned his companions, he was hit by another Messerschmitt that he had not seen. As his Hurricane was hit, Fowler turned into a steep dive following a Messerschmitt that had flashed past on his left. He shot down the Bf 109 but was again attacked by another Messerschmitt. Fowler managed to turn his aircraft over and open the canopy before falling out and parachuting to the ground.

Landing among trees in the Ardennes Forest, Fowler joined a group of French engineers who had been mining bridges during the retreat, but in due course they ran into German tanks in a village from which there was no escape. Fowler was sent to Stalag Luft 1 at Barth, from where he managed to escape and make his way to the Baltic coast. He was arrested again at Sassnitz and sent to camp Oflag IV-C at Colditz, the highest-security PoW camp. He succeeded in escaping again and made his way to Switzerland.[25]

Consignment to Colditz might be regarded as an inverted accolade for escapers and evaders. They were sent there either because they were a high-status prisoner or because they had a habit of getting out of less secure camps. However, it was even better if, when you bailed out of a plane and managed to avoid German soldiers on the ground, you then fell into the hands of an escape organisation. This is highlighted by the fortunes of different crew members of

102 Squadron Handley Page Halifax II W7653 'DY-A' after taking off from RAF Dalton in North Yorkshire at 2138 on 27 April 1942.

While most people might enjoy a clear moonlit night, for the crew of an RAF bomber during the crossing over the French coast and into occupied Europe it was several times more unpleasant and dangerous than an electric storm. Although the Mk II version of the Halifax was powered by the excellent Merlin XX, the engines that were used on the Avro Lancaster, the Halifax was bigger and heavier than the Lancaster and the engines were not powerful enough to allow it to climb out of the range of night fighters. Later the Halifax would be fitted with more powerful Bristol Hercules engines capable of dealing with its size and weight. That was then; this was now. The eerie silence was accentuated by the absence of flak. This was an ominous sign as it often meant that the flak gunners were holding their fire in order not to hit one of their own night fighters. Sure enough, a dark shape flitted across the blazing white of the moon, like a shark in the ocean. Soon cannon shells were ploughing into the fuselage of the Halifax.

The rear gunner, George 'Dixie' Lee, managed to shoot down the Bf 110 after it had attacked again but the damage was done. The Halifax went into a steep dive and the pilot, Flight Sergeant Lawrence 'Larry' Carr, ordered the crew to bail out. Carr had already jumped before Dixie Lee had managed to struggle out of his gun position and get out of the aircraft as it careered towards the ground. Two of the crew were killed and four were made PoWs.*

Lee landed with a thud in a field near to the plane wreck. The village of Hamois was fairly close to where he had landed and he headed towards it. He was greeted by friendly villagers; however, there was a German collaborator among them who reported his presence to the German authorities, and he was soon arrested.

Larry Carr had a similar miraculous escape with barely enough time for the parachute to deploy before he hit the ground. Having hidden his parachute and lifejacket, Carr headed south away from the

---

* Sgt Ronald Barry, W/O George Henry, Flt Sgt James Ralston and Sgt Ivor Edwards were all captured and became prisoners of war. Sgt James Garroway and Flt Sgt Kenneth Robinson were both killed in action. Flt Sgt Larry Carr escaped over the Pyrenees with the Comet line and returned to England via Gibraltar.

wreck, using an escape compass to guide him. As he walked away, he was spotted by two Belgians who had seen the crash. They were Constable Louis Massinon, a local gendarme, and Mauritius Wilmet. Both were members of the Comet escape line. Having asked Carr whether he wanted to return to England and having received an enthusiastic 'yes', they guided him to Wilmet's house at Hamois, where he was concealed in the basement. After providing him with a meal, his helpers guided him to a farm a few kilometres away and he was provided with civilian clothes. The next morning Carr got onto a train with Wilmet to Ciney, south-east of Namur. There they rendezvoused with a young woman called Fernande Pirlot, or Pochette, who accompanied them on a train to Brussels.[26]

Once he had arrived in the Belgian capital, Carr was taken to the first of many safe houses that he would stay in during the weeks ahead. Pochette was always on hand to act as a guide and courier while also arranging essentials such as the new identity card. Another helper, Peggy van Lier, or Marguerite, took Carr to a safe house owned by Carl Servais while news came in that the Germans had arrested several members of the Comet line. The news did not deter Carr's helpers and on 20 May van Lier escorted Carr to the Gare du Nord in Brussels, where he was introduced to a young woman who exuded radiant determination. Her name was Andrée de Jongh.

1

The Three Ds

Having been brought up in avenue Émile Verhaeren in Schaerbeek by her father Paul, a principal at a local primary school, and her mother Alice, along with her sister Suzanne, Andrée de Jongh, also known as Dédée, started her career as a poster designer before training as a nurse. There are obvious links of location and vocation tying her to Edith Cavell, not to mention the almost identical circumstances of a German invasion about thirty years after the one experienced by her compatriots in the First World War.

Andrée was not alone in her determination to do something to help once German jackboots had resounded through the streets of Brussels and once a German military administration began to be established under General Alexander von Falkenhausen. Many Belgians had spontaneously helped either Allied soldiers to escape after the evacuations to England or Allied airmen who had been brought down in early defensive battles. It had become apparent, however, that the freelance help offered by generous-minded local citizens to evading Allied servicemen had its limitations and obvious dangers. They could not provide a co-ordinated escape route and, as the Germans became more established in occupied countries, the danger to both evaders and helpers grew exponentially.

Belgian Resistance Movements

Belgian resistance during the Second World War has not received
the same attention given to the movement in France. This may be
partly explained by the fact that it lacked a figurehead such as the
French had in General de Gaulle. Instead, the Belgian Government
in exile was at odds with King Leopold, who had surrendered to
the Germans in order to save Belgian lives. On the other hand, the
people of Belgium largely blamed the Government in exile for the
chaos in Belgium.

As the dust began to settle after the German invasion and the evacuation of British and other Allied forces from Dunkirk, the German
Militärverwaltung was imposed to replace Belgian administration and
gradually the process of registering the Jewish population and the
issue of spurious 'letters of employment' led in due course to the
deportation of Jews in August 1942. The horrific implications of
what was happening to the Jewish population led to a growing effort
by Belgian citizens to do something about it, or, in other words, to
resist. This included efforts by the Catholic community to register
Jewish children in Catholic schools, while individual priests sheltered
Jews wherever they could be hidden. Father Joseph André,[1] a chaplain to parishes in Niemen, provided temporary shelter for Jews until
more permanent arrangements could be made. His immediate neigh-
bour was the German Kommandantur. However, rather than being
just passive recipients of help, the Jews themselves became active
participants in underground and clandestine movements and activities. The Committee for the Defence of the Jews, founded by Hertz
Jospa and Have Groisman, which was linked to the Independent
Front resistance organisation, was set up and succeeded in rescuing
thousands of Jews, including 2,500 children.[2]

An exponential increase in resistance activity was a direct result
of the introduction of compulsory employment in Germany, which
was enacted from 8 October 1942. Large numbers of men went into
hiding and as a result became dependent on a network of helpers to
shelter and feed them. In response to this development, the Belgian
Government in London set up an organisation called Socrates to
support the men evading forced labour. It is thought to have saved

about 40,000 men from deportation. Most resistance organisations, however, grew from the ground upwards. They included the White Brigade, formed in 1940 by Marcel Louette, a schoolteacher who built the brigade around liberal youth movements.[3] The White Brigade provided information to the Belgian Government in London about German military movements and establishments, intelligence about V-bomb sites and tips on German agents. Based largely in the port of Antwerp, the White Brigade would play an important role during the relief of the port when British and Canadian forces advanced eastwards. Its members were experts in sabotage, including cutting telephone wires and dynamiting bridges, but during the relief of Antwerp their role was reversed when they countered German sabotage efforts and thus helped to keep the port intact so that it could be used by Allied shipping for vital resupply of the advancing forces. As with most resistance organisations, the White Brigade became a target for Gestapo counter-resistance measures and eighty-one of its 125 leaders were arrested, interrogated under torture and either sent to concentration camps or executed.

Formed largely of Belgian ex-military personnel, the Secret Army, also known as the Belgian Légion, was created by the merger of two separate paramilitary organisations. Like other resistance movements, it saw a rapid increase in recruitment following the official forced labour order in October 1942. The Secret Army was split into three major zones covering Flanders, Brussels and Wallonia.[4]

The Independent Front was formed from the clandestine Communist Party of Belgium and grew to become a broad church of socialists and liberals. The Independent Front had a strong presence in Brussels and in industrial areas, and much of its work was focused on helping the families of resistance fighters who had been arrested by the Nazis as well as evaders in safe houses. It also made a significant contribution to the thriving clandestine forces in Belgium.

The Communist Party was also the foundation of the armed partisans, a movement that resulted from the German invasion of the Soviet Union in 1941.

One of the most significant aspects of the Belgian resistance movement, as it had been during the First World War, was the clandestine press. The Communist Party produced a newspaper called

Le Drapeau Rouge, while other newspapers included *La Libre Belgique*, *Le Voix des Belges*, *Le Clandestin* and the *Front*, which was one of the most widely distributed. As the German authorities had censored the regular press, some journalists moved to the underground press, where they could express their opinions freely until the Gestapo caught up with them. Writers included Robert Logelan, under the pen name Peter Pan, and Paul Struye.

The impact of the clandestine press was not lost on the Gestapo and by July 1943 they managed to locate the printing press for *Le Drapeau Rouge*. Rather than shut it down, the Gestapo continued to publish editions with messaging that served their purposes. The clandestine press retaliated by publishing their own edition of one of the authorised newspapers, *Le Soir*, containing news and editorials that would not have passed the Nazi censor. The authorities clamped down again and thirty-two members of the Belgian resistance were arrested and deported to concentration camps from which they never returned.

The resistance battle was also fought on the airwaves. Belgian broadcasters such as the National Institute for Radio Broadcasts (NIR) strove to keep their voice. Transmitters were run underground in Belgium, while some were moved to France. However, the main way of communicating with the resistance was through the BBC. Listening to it was forbidden by the authorities but a resistance mission destroyed the records of radio owners in Belgium, making it impossible for the authorities to track them down. It was via the BBC that the resistance could receive coded messages about agent insertions or collections as well as supply drops.

Another significant resistance organisation was Groupe G, or Groupe général de Sabotage de Belgique. As its name suggests, Groupe G had a clear mission to cause as much disruption as possible to the German authorities and it was highly successful. It was formed by students of the Free University of Brussels, leading members of whom were Jean Bergers and André Wendelin. Groupe G worked in co-ordination with the Special Operations Executive (SOE) and was based in Brussels, Liège and Namur. Leaders of the various groups travelled to England to receive training in sabotage techniques or radio communications. They were then parachuted back into Belgium once they had achieved a standard of proficiency whereby they could teach others. Equipment for Groupe G was also parachuted into Belgium by SOE, which gave them the raw materials to carry out their operations. Having been trained in Britain and supplied with the equipment they needed, Groupe G became a formidable force and their sabotage exploits ranged from destroying twenty-eight electricity pylons in January 1944 to sabotaging twenty-nine locomotives in August the same year. After the Allied landings in Normandy, Groupe G continued to work in co-operation with Allied forces to disrupt railways and electrical networks.

Commander Charles Claser had helped found the Belgian Légion in July 1941. In July 1942 he travelled to England, where he worked with Commander Henri Bernard, who was head of the 2nd Section, and with members of the SOE to draw up plans for a possible Allied landing on the Belgian coast. On his return to Belgium, Claser set up a separate organisation, the Corps Franc Belge d'Action Militaire. The CFBAM was divided into two sections, one of which included direct action operations and the other sabotage. However, German intelligence had got wind of the arrangements and the Gestapo moved in to break up the plans. Many resistance members were arrested and either executed or sent to concentration camps. Claser was sent to Gross-Rosen concentration camp, where he died. In response, London sent out another leader in the form of Colonel Bastin to set up a new resistance organisation called the Armée Belgique. In due course, Bastin was also arrested and was replaced by Colonel Ivan Gerard. He was eventually compromised but managed to escape to England. Lieutenant General Jules Pire then took command until the liberation of Belgium by the Allies.

In July 1943 a Captain Adelin Marissal was parachuted into France with instructions for the Armée Belge. These included the 'Trojan Horse' plans for the organisation and direction of military resistance. It also included a plan for sabotage and actions on D-Day. The D-Day plan of action included sabotage to delay German reinforcements as well as direct action against German forces. On 1 June 1944 a coded message over the BBC was a warning order for Secret Army members to take up their positions. Another coded message signalled the resistance fighters to disable the railways, engines and rolling stock, destroy bridges and sabotage communications. To help co-ordinate these operations, Major William (Bill) Fraser and three members of the Belgian Special Air Service (SAS) were dropped by parachute.

Apart from Edith Cavell, Andrée de Jongh was also inspired by the witness of a homegrown heroine, Camille Petit. A working-class girl born in Tournai in 1893, Petit was 21 when the First World War began and the Germans occupied her homeland. She escorted her fiancé across the Dutch border after he had been wounded and, having offered information about the German occupiers to the British, she was soon recruited by British intelligence. She continued to pass on information to the British about German troop move-ments while also distributing the clandestine newspaper *La Libre Belgique*. Like Cavell, she continued to help Allied soldiers who were wounded or evading capture to cross the Dutch border.

Petit was arrested in February 1916, having been betrayed. After imprisonment in St-Gilles prison, she was tried and sentenced to death. She was executed at the Tir National on 1 April 1916.

Unlike Edith Cavell, whose trial and execution attracted wide-spread international attention and condemnation, Petit remained relatively unknown until after the war, when she was celebrated as a working-class national heroine. She was awarded a state funeral in May 1919 that was attended by Queen Elizabeth of Belgium, the Catholic Cardinal Nercier and the Belgian Prime Minister Léon Delacroix. The funeral included a burial with full military honours at Schaerbeek cemetery, where her name is listed on a plaque that includes the name E. Cavell.

Andrée de Jongh's extraordinary efforts in organising the escape line and motivating others had a missionary-like fervour. Although she was not brought up in a formal religious tradition, it is clear she was inspired by those who gave themselves for others. Edith Cavell and Gabrielle Petit were themselves examples of this kind of heroic witness but de Jongh was also inspired by Saint Damien de Veuster (1840–89), a Belgian Catholic priest and missionary who ministered to lepers in the then Kingdom of Hawaii. This was to be de Jongh's destiny after the war when she returned, barely alive, from a German concentration camp. It also helps to explain her eventual adoption of the Catholic faith. De Jongh was perhaps not the sort of person who would have been persuaded by religious doctrine alone. Her journey to faith was a long and complex one that would be influenced by the many challenges she would encounter over the coming years.

Dédée's personal determination to help was shared by her friend, Arnold Deppé, and by his cousin, Henri de Bliqui. Deppé was familiar with the Basque region, having worked with a film company based at the coastal port of St-Jean-de-Luz and at San Sebastián. He also had a contact there, Elvire de Greef, a Belgian woman who had travelled south with her husband and two children, Frederick and Janine, to evade the fighting in the north and in the hope of escaping to England. The family had then decided to settle in the area, buying a villa at Anglet. Elvire de Greef, whose code name became Tante Go, was to prove a key link in the Comet line in the south. She was both resourceful and possessed of a steely determination to move mountains in the cause of freedom and justice. Her husband, Fernand, had a job in local government where he acted as a translator for the German Army. This gave him an opportunity to forge documents to aid evaders. The de Greef family were accompanied by an English chauffeur called Albert Edward Johnson, code-named 'B'.

Deppé had other contacts in the area whom he recruited to help with escape arrangements, including Alejandro Elizalde and two guides, Manuel Iturrioz and Tomas Arabitarte. These latter two men would pioneer the first escapes before Florentino Goikoetxea became the primary guide for the Comet evasion missions over the Pyrenees.

In early 1941, there were more organised efforts to help and house British soldiers, some of whom had taken refuge in the Forêt de Soignes. Georges Marie Guillon, owner of a carpet company, provided significant help in the late summer of 1940 and the network he created began to grow. The director of the SOFINA company, Baron Jaques Donny, brought Allied servicemen to Brussels and organised safe houses and finance. He also arranged through his various contacts, including the owner of a clothes shop, for the evaders to be provided with civilian clothing.

In April 1941, de Bliqui was arrested by the Gestapo. He was one of the early victims of the Nazi collaborator Prosper Dezitter, who had managed to infiltrate the organisation. Dédée and Arnold Deppé continued to develop their plans and in July 1941 they set out from Brussels with their first party, consisting of Belgian servicemen who wanted to join Belgian forces in England, and a secret agent working for the Allies called Frederique Alice Dupuich, otherwise known as Miss Richards.[5]

Dédée and Deppé had decided to travel separately on the journey south and they sat in different carriages of the train from Brussels to Lille. The route had been planned meticulously. Dédée would travel with her party as far as Quiévrain, before crossing the Belgian–French border. Two more changes of train would get them to Corbie, where they would face the challenge of crossing the river Somme undetected. Deppé had arranged with a local farmer's wife, Renée Boulanger, known as Nenette, for a boat to be concealed in rushes on the Belgian side, which they would use to get across the river.

Having reached Corbie, they had a meal to recover from their long journey, encumbered by the large amount of luggage that Miss Richards had brought with her, and waited until dusk so that there was less risk of being seen. Deppé then led them towards the banks of the Somme and, leaving the main party concealed among some trees, he went forward to reconnoitre the riverbank and find the boat. As he approached the river, he noticed a red glow, which he soon identified as a campfire around which were seated a group of people enjoying the summer night. Unfortunately, their camp site was almost on top of the place where the boat was moored.

Deppé returned to the group to inform them that they had no choice but to swim across the river. Dédée told him that at least seven of the party could not swim and that they would therefore have to devise some form of swimming aid. While Deppé went off to find something buoyant, de Jongh went forward to recce the river herself, though she had to conceal herself quickly when she saw the lamp on a bicycle that proved to belong to a German sentry on patrol.[6]

Deppé returned with a long length of wire and the inner tube of a car tyre. After avoiding another German bicycle sentry, he tied the end of the wire round a tree and swam across the river with the free end, accompanied by Dédée. Once he had reached the other side, Dédée swam back to collect the first passenger. She repeated the swim across and back several times until everyone was over. The most challenging passenger proved to be Miss Richards, whose suitcase had to be carried over on a plank and who had to be persuaded to strip down to her underwear. At the vital moment, another German bicycle sentry appeared and Dédée had to force Miss Richards to conceal herself by getting into the river. They then swam across.[7]

As they recovered at Nenette's farmhouse, Dédée and Deppé realised that the swimming episode, despite its humorous moments, had been too close for comfort. Despite the disarming air of unreality on a warm summer's night with a campfire and holidaymakers nearby, if any of the frequent German patrols had spotted them, they would have faced prison, interrogation and the prospect of deportation to a concentration camp. Having dried their clothes, and replenished by food and sleep, the party set off again, taking a train via Amiens to Paris. Here they stayed in safe houses before catching an overnight train to Bayonne in south-west France, one of the principal cities of the Basque country. From there they moved south-west to Anglet, a fashionable commune near the sea, not far from Biarritz. Their destination was the Villa Voisin, the home of Elvire and Fernand de Greef and their two children, Frederick and Janine. The determined and energetic Elvire soon arranged safe houses in the area for the party of evaders until the time came for them to be guided across the Pyrenees mountains. She provided them with the best food available, some of it obtained via the black market. Dédée and Deppé accompanied the party to the Spanish border and then turned back the way they had come. However, all did not go well for the evaders. Once across the border, they were stopped by Spanish Guardias Civiles. The three Belgian servicemen were escorted back over the border and handed over to the German authorities before being sent to concentration camps.

2

Trial Run

In many ways, the first evasion journey had been a success. Dédée and Deppé had managed to reconnoitre a route, set up staging posts at vital points, surmount the obstacle posed by the river Somme and pass unnoticed with their evaders until they reached the Spanish border. However, like most first endeavours, it had its learning points. For Dédée it became clear that she must escort her evaders all the way on the other side of the border. Although she was a civilian in her twenties and her evaders were highly trained servicemen, they were mostly unable to communicate in the local language and had none of the contacts that Dédée and her Comet line helpers could provide.

Dédée had thought further about her experience. In her view, taking a train through Lille would expose the evaders to intense security checks, increasing the chance of something going wrong. For her next trip, she planned to take a more circuitous route to Quiévrain via Mons and then cross the frontier into France on foot. Then she planned to catch a train to Valenciennes, where she would change to the train for Corbie. Meanwhile, Deppé decided to take the more straightforward route through Lille, with disastrous consequences.

Having planned to escort three British servicemen, Private James (Jim) Cromar of the 1st Gordon Highlanders, Corporal Enoch Bettley and Private Samuel Slavin, de Jongh discovered that two of them had been arrested in their lodgings in Schaerbeek in Brussels.

They were taken to St-Gilles prison, where they were interrogated and beaten before being sent to a PoW camp in Germany. Cromar would be the lucky one. He had been arrested along with others of the 51st Highland Division at St-Valery-en-Caux and he had tried to escape while on the march towards captivity by diving into a canal. However, he almost drowned and had to be rescued by a German guard.[1] He would make good his escape at a later date. De Jongh decided to offer the two other places to two Belgian officers, called Robert Merchiers and Ernest Sterckmans. Meanwhile, Deppé boarded the Lille train with six Belgians. Little did he know that he had been betrayed by a man who worked at La Libre Belgique for a mere 200 francs. It also proved to be a close call for Dédée, who had climbed on to Deppé's train in order to have a last conversation about their plans, including a rendezvous at Corbie. Neither of them guessed that they were being followed by the Gestapo. Once they had finished their conversation, Dédée got off the Lille train and went over to the train alongside, unnoticed by the Gestapo agents. Once Dédée and her charges had arrived at Corbie, they got off the train to await Deppé's arrival, but he did not appear. By then, he had been arrested at Lille.

Having waited several hours, Dédée and her group crossed the river Somme and found safe harbour at Nenette's farmhouse on the other side. Leaving her wards in Nenette's care, Dédée then crossed the river and caught a train to Lille to try to find out what had happened to Deppé. Unable to obtain any information as to his whereabouts, she returned to the farmhouse to pick up the three men and continued to Paris. Here they stayed in a safe house where Dédée received a coded letter from Elvire de Greef warning her that there were strict customs checks at Bayonne for anyone arriving from outside the region. To make matters worse, Deppé had the false papers they would need, and Dédée was running out of money. However, they owed their continuing safety to the fact that Deppé refused to divulge any information about their movements, despite being interrogated by the Gestapo.

Having eventually rendezvoused with Elvire de Greef, they were introduced to their Basque guide, Tomas. The guide was sceptical about their chances of completing the journey in view of the arduous nature of the terrain and the challenge of crossing the Bidassoa river. Nevertheless, they set off and having climbed the mountain and descended into the valley, they managed to cross the river. Having climbed another steep slope, they came upon a disued farm building, where they waited throughout the next day, ready to move again at night fall. There was no food available, and they continued their journey on empty stomachs, tired from the previous night's efforts and with the prospect of another long, hard walk ahead of them. For another eight hours they slogged uphill and down until at last they reached a farm in Guipuzcoa, by which time they were exhausted. The guide Tomas suddenly announced that he was leaving. Andrée forcefully pointed out that he was contracted to take them the whole way but he told her that he had arranged for someone to come up from San Sebastián to guide them for the rest of the journey. They slept in a flea-infested farm hut, while the farmer's wife provided them with stew and milk. Eventually, the new guide Bernardo Aracama arrived and led them to San Sebastián, where he took them to his apartment. His wife Antonia had prepared a substantial meal. While de Jongh and the three men slept off their exhaustion, Antonia washed all their clothes and dried them overnight in a nearby baker's oven. The guide explained to de Jongh that the British consul was based in Bilbao and that there was only a vice-consul in San Sebastián. Dédée was concerned about travelling to Bilbao with the men on the train, but the guide reassured her that they would be all right if they caught the early train as it was full of people heading to market and there were few checks.

Having travelled the 100km by train to Bilbao without event, Dédée and the three men then walked to the British consulate. They were met by a well-dressed young man, who escorted Colin Cromar to a separate room. When Dédée asked to see the consul, she was told that he was away but that she could see the vice-consul, Arthur Dean. She was taken to a room where a man with fine features asked her to sit down. For some reason she guessed by his appearance and demeanour that he was an ex-naval officer. He invited her to talk while he filled a pipe with tobacco. Dédée told him everything about their journey while he puffed thoughtfully on the pipe. When she had finished, Dean repeated what he had understood and then asked why she was there. She explained that she wanted to establish an escape line for all the Allied servicemen in Belgium. Tapping his pipe on an ashtray, Dean told her that he would need to think about it and asked her to return the next day. Cromar was allowed to stay at the consulate and, as Dédée prepared to leave with the two Belgians, he grasped her hand and said, 'God bless you!'[2]

Dédée and the Belgians stayed the night in a local hotel and she was back the next day. Dean asked her more questions and told her that no decisions had yet been made. The process went on for three days while a decision was awaited from the British Embassy in Madrid. Eventually, she was told that someone from the embassy had arrived to meet her. The new visitor was Michael Creswell, first secretary at the British Embassy in Madrid.

While Dédée had been kept waiting, there had been much correspondence between the British Embassy in Madrid and the intelligence services in London, including the head of MI6, Sir Claude Dansey. Some thought Dédée might be a plant by the Nazis and that she should be treated with caution. However, the consular officials in Spain had formed a different opinion. Impressed with her simplicity and courage, they also had the evidence of Cromar, who had sung her praises when he was debriefed.

Dédée returned to France, where she told Elvire de Greef about the latest developments. She in turn was informed by Elvire that Arnold Deppé had been arrested. Another helper, a French officer called Charles Morelle, advised Dédée not to return to Brussels as she would almost certainly be arrested and he offered her the use of his house in Valenciennes, just over the Franco-Belgian border. This could be a staging post for evacuations. Elvire offered to travel to Brussels in Dédée's place to pick up two more evaders, Robert Conville and Alan Cowan.

Once Elvire had arrived in Brussels and contacted the two British servicemen, they caught the train from Brussels on 14 November. All was going well until the train reached Quiévrain where, under the eye of a German Feldgendarm, French customs officials accosted Elvire and the two men. They asked Elvire what relationship she had with the men, and she explained that she had met them by chance and, discovering that they were Flemish and could not speak French, had offered to accompany them so that she could translate for them. The two Scotsmen were ushered into an office, where a customs official asked them to empty their pockets. A pile of cigarette packets was produced but also some identity cards. The customs official disappeared for a while and Bobby Conville took the opportunity to start stuffing the cigarettes back into his pocket, to the amusement of the German guard. Bobby then left the room, telling Alan to wait for the official. Elvire then signalled frantically for Alan to get out as well and he soon followed. As the three of them hurried away, they heard a shout behind them. It was the French customs official and he was smiling broadly. He handed back some of the cigarettes he had confiscated and also returned their identity cards. These were false Flemish identity cards but also their British Army ID cards. Despite the warnings they had been given before travelling, the two men were carrying incriminating documents. The customs official told Elvire that he would have been paid 60,000 francs for handing over the two British soldiers to the Germans. He then bade them farewell and cycled off.

Fortunately, the German guard had regarded the incident as a case of petty smuggling of cigarettes and had not spotted the incriminating ID cards. It was equally fortunate that the French customs official was pro-British and chose not to report them. His loyalty to the cause of freedom was greater than his urge for personal gain. If it had gone the other way, the men would have faced spending the rest of the war in a PoW camp and Elvire would have been interrogated and tortured prior to execution or deportation to a concentration camp. The link she provided for the Comet line in the south would have been compromised. The incident also highlighted the extraordinary presence of mind of the Comet line guides when faced with potentially compromising incidents. Elvire managed to spin a story about why she was in the company of the two men and she also saw the opportunity for the men to get away once the official's back was turned.[3]

Once Robert Colville and Alan Cowan had rendezvoused with Dédée at Valenciennes, she helped them cross the river Somme by boat and led them to Nenette's farmhouse before guiding them to Amiens and Paris and then on to Bayonne. Here they caught a bus to St-Jean-de-Luz. Dédée then accompanied the two men across the Pyrenees with the Basque guide Florentino Goikoetxea. Florentino was a true man of the mountains with a mountainous build who could find his way around even in the darkest nights and most severe weather. They reached San Sebastián on 16 October and Dédée then accompanied them on the train to Bilbao, where they reached the British consulate.

By this time, any remaining doubts that the British authorities may have had about Andrée de Jongh's motives had been allayed. Here were two more British servicemen safely delivered and singing her praises. What more evidence did they need? Thoughts had now moved on to how this nascent escape line could become more firmly established and what sort of financial arrangements needed to be made. Dédée's first meeting with the British diplomat Michael Creswell had gone well and he would become her most important link in Spain. He was largely instrumental in finding a way through some of the obstacles in the higher levels of British intelligence and diplomatic circles. Described as a large, warm man, Creswell worked for the British Directorate of Military Intelligence Section 9 (MI9) with the code name Monday. It was an advantage for Dédée that he also spoke perfect French. Creswell enjoyed the high life, was fond of sport and cars and had reported to British intelligence on the activities of Hermann Göring while he was based in Germany in 1939. It was fortunate that Creswell enjoyed driving because he would be very busy over the coming months picking up evaders from near the Spanish–French border and driving them via Madrid to Gibraltar, often using his own car, a 1940s Bentley. This provided a vital and efficient link that would speed evaders back to Britain.

Creswell proposed to Dédée that the British Government would pay any expenses she incurred in bringing out Allied servicemen. Dédée agreed but said that any money would be paid back after the war. In the circumstances, this was an extraordinary assertion of independence. It was also a signal that, for all their willingness to collaborate in the name of the Allied cause, Dédée and the other Comet line helpers would continue to keep British intelligence at arm's length.

After helping the members of the beleaguered Highland Division to evade, Dédée received her first RAF evaders. These were two Englishmen, Howard Carroll and Jack Newton, and an Australian, Hilary Birk. Although only 20 years old, Carroll was already a second lieutenant, while Newton was a charming young sergeant, already married to his sweetheart, Mary. Hilary, or Larry, was a typical product of an Australian sheep farm. Newton had been a rear gunner in a Vickers Wellington II of 12 Squadron operating out of RAF Binbrook in the Lincolnshire Wolds in what is now an Area of Outstanding Natural Beauty. The medium bomber took off at 2225 on 5 August 1941 before taking an easterly course over the North Sea and crossing the Dutch coast on its journey towards its target in Germany. On the return trip, it appears that the aircraft was hit by flak but the pilot, Flight Lieutenant B. Langlois, retained enough control to carry out an emergency landing at Antwerpen-Deurne airport. Fortunately, the airport was deserted, and the crew managed to get out safely before setting light to the aircraft.

In order to minimise the chances of capture, the men decided to split into two groups of three and set off in different directions. Newton's group was lucky enough to be spotted by a member of the Belgian resistance, who put them in touch with a Comet line agent. Soon they were on their way to Brussels, where they were split up and allocated separate safe houses. Over the next five months, Newton was moved around and given safe haven by about forty different families, all of whom were risking dire repercussions from the Nazis should they have been discovered. Eventually, Newton was handed over to the capable hands of de Jongh and in early December began his journey south towards the Pyrenees, along with his English and Australian companions.

Once they had reached the foothills and been prepared for the trek ahead, they eventually reached the Bidassoa river, but found that it was in spate and too dangerous to cross. Desperate to get back to see his young wife, Newton said he would be crossing anyway, and on his own if necessary, until Dédée gave him a military command to rejoin the rest of the group.[4] The rain poured down upon them and the frozen grass was as slippery as an ice rink as they made their way back to the small farm where they had found refuge. The next day, the river continued to be in spate and the guides told them that they could cross at a bridge some distance away. The detour took several hours, and they eventually reached a bridge by a waterfall that was illuminated by electric lights and known to be patrolled by Spanish Guardias Civiles. However, luck was on their side and they managed to cross unseen.

Once Dédée had safely delivered her first batch of airmen, she returned immediately to Valenciennes where another 'package' of four RAF airmen arrived – one Canadian and three Englishmen. They reached Tante Go's house by Christmas Eve, where they spent a cheerful evening singing along to carols on the BBC.[5]

MI9 and the European
Escape Lines

There was a reason why the British authorities were initially cautious about welcoming Andrée de Jongh with open arms. Dédée's arrival in Bilbao followed closely on the near collapse of the Pat O'Leary line, which had been instrumental in helping many Allied servicemen to escape to Spain.

Working in the relative safety of Vichy France, businessman Nubar Gulbenkian, son of Calouste Gulbenkian, had begun to organise an escape line from Vichy France over the border to Barcelona and the Scottish soldier Ian Garrow energetically set about organising groups of volunteers who would form the basis of the chain that escorted the Allied airmen to the south. Garrow served in the Highland Light Infantry and had managed to escape imprisonment by the Germans after the Highland 51st Division had been forced to surrender on 12 June 1940. He had made his way south to Marseille, where he was nominally interned by the Vichy regime.

Pat O'Leary was the alias of Albert Guerisse, a Belgian officer who had escaped to England at the time of the Dunkirk evacuations and who had been trained by British intelligence. He took part in covert sabotage operations on the French south coast on the Royal Navy special service vessel HMS *Fidelity*, which was a converted French merchant vessel used for SOE missions such as agent drops and collections and sabotage. Guerisse was commissioned as a Royal Navy Volunteer Reserve (RNVR) lieutenant commander with the name of Albert O'Leary. The captain of the ship, Claude

Peri, was also given a Royal Naval Reserve commission. His mistress, Madeleine Bayard, was commissioned in the Women's Royal Naval Service (WRNS) as Madeleine Barclay. During an operation, Guerisse was separated from his ship and was arrested on the coast by Vichy police. Ian Garrow heard about his imprisonment and arranged a rescue operation, after which Guerisse, or Pat O'Leary, joined Garrow's organisation.

Like the Comet line, the Pat O'Leary line took airmen who had been shot down over northern Europe, sheltered and clothed them and provided them with false papers before escorting them via several routes over the north-east Spanish border. However, due to its open and voluntary nature, the O'Leary line was also prone to infiltration by the German authorities, who used traitors and informers, some of whom gained the confidence of the administrators of the line before striking. During his work helping evaders, Garrow was arrested by the Vichy police in October 1941. Guerisse then took over the escape line operations and members of the line rescued Garrow from prison in December 1942. Garrow was sheltered in Toulouse before crossing the Pyrenees and finding sanctuary at the British Embassy in Barcelona. He returned to England in February 1943. Guerisse proved to be one of the most consequential of the European escape and evasion organisers and, along with Andrée de Jongh, a guiding star of the Belgian resistance. Like Dédée, he showed initiative and leadership qualities in organising the escape line but, unlike her, he had been trained in undercover operations in England.

After his arrest by the Germans, Guerisse was tortured by the Gestapo but refused to give away the names of the organisers and helpers of the escape line. He was then sent to various concentration camps, including Mauthausen and Natzweiler-Struthof, where he witnessed the execution of four SOE female agents: Diana Rowden, Sonya Olschanezky, Andrée Borrel and Vera Leigh.[1] He was then moved to Dachau, where he was again tortured and sentenced to death. However, he narrowly missed the death penalty as the Allies advanced and the camp guards surrendered.

In due course, the British intelligence escape bureau MI9 took over the costs of the Comet line operations and provided other forms of support. Military Intelligence Section 9 was established on

23 December 1939 to provide support for British and Commonwealth escapers and evaders. It was partly inspired by a similar organisation of the First World War called MI IA but was effectively an entirely new unit. In its early days, part of MI9 dealt with captured enemy prisoners but this became part of a separate organisation from 1941 so that MI9 was fully devoted to escape and evasion. MI9 was located in Room 424 of the Metropole Hotel in Northumberland Avenue and was headed by Major N.R. Crockatt. MI9's responsibilities included training officers in escape and evasion techniques, which they were expected to pass on to their men. The training was carried out at Intelligence School 9 (IS9) in Highgate, north London. An MI9 department also created escape aids, including maps printed on fabric or silk, covert compasses and specialised knives and other tools. MI9 had reasonably good relations with the SOE, headed by Brigadier Colin Gubbins. The Secret Intelligence Service (SIS) maintained links with MI9 in its work in north-west Europe, mainly through the SIS contact Jimmy Langley when he returned to England from France in early 1941.

MI9 operations covered all Allied personnel and initially the Americans placed a liaison officer in MI9 to handle the affairs of the US 8th Air Force, which was their major aerial arm in northern Europe. The liaison officer dispensed escape kits and other materials to US airmen operating from the United Kingdom and also supervised training in escape and evasion. The Americans also set up their own escape and evasion section based on MI9 that was called Military Intelligence Section X (MIS-X). Like MI9, MIS-X provided both training and tools to be used by downed American airmen and by prisoners of war. Special escape and evasion kits were concealed in aid packages sent to PoW camps to enable them to escape and to survive after escape. Whether downed in enemy territory or captured by the enemy, American and British and Commonwealth servicemen had a mutual interest in escape and this was reflected in the high levels of co-operation between the British and American escape organisations and officials.

The Pat O'Leary line was infiltrated by a British traitor called Harold Cole. He had been introduced to the Marseille side of the operation by the British servicemen Rolan Lepers, who had personally escorted many airmen to safety. Cole was put in charge of the Lille end of the Pat O'Leary operation but it soon became apparent that he was using the expenses that were meant to cover escape costs for his own ends. Cole was arrested by the Germans in December 1941 and he provided them with the details of many of the Pat line workers. However, Cole was not the only traitor to damage the Pat line. Roger le Neveu was another helper who was recruited by the Germans and betrayed Guerisse.

The MI9 contact in London for the Pat O'Leary line was Airey Neave, who was himself familiar with the art of escaping. Neave was the first PoW to escape from the high-security prison Oflag IV-C at Colditz Castle. He had previously escaped from Stalag XX-A at Toruń in Poland. However, he was captured while trying to reach Soviet-controlled Poland and imprisoned again at Colditz, which had the highest levels of security. Having tried and failed to escape a first time, he tried again along with a Dutch officer and this time he was successful. The two men managed to cross the Swiss border and Neave then found his way through France to Spain and then Gibraltar. When he was appointed to MI9, he was closely involved in helping other escapers and evaders to follow similar routes to freedom.

Neave understood that, as time went on, established escape lines that had a relaxed approach to security, or which recruited helpers without adequate screening, were more prone to attack and that new blood and new lines were needed to keep one step ahead of the Gestapo and its network of informers. To keep things tight and secure, MI9 focused on developing more compact escape routes, sometimes by sea or air, which were run by trained intelligence operators. These would include the Shelburne and Possum escape lines.

Against this background, the arrival of Andrée de Jongh in Bilbao and her suggestion of operating an escape line between Belgium and the Spanish border caused conflicting emotions among the British intelligence authorities. An escape route for downed airmen was certainly necessary but was this to be another debacle leading to the arrest and incarceration of helpers and servicemen? However, there was something about Dédée that won over even the most sceptical diplomats and intelligence officials, and Neave was no exception. Like Creswell, he would be charmed by her ingenuous spirit and determination and was resolved to give her as much help as he could.

However, after the experience of the Pat O'Leary line, Neave was very concerned about the lack of communication between MI9 and the organisers of the Comet line, other than the occasional handover meetings with Michael Creswell at Bilbao. He knew that, as time went on, de Jongh and her father would become ever more exposed to danger and he was proven right. However, Dédée and the Comet line survived not because of its contacts with British intelligence but due to the fierce independence and loyalty that Dédée and her cause inspired in all of its organisers and helpers. The Comet line worked in collaboration with MI9 but it was not dependent on it.

Even if British intelligence had been more involved in Comet operations than it was, it is difficult to see how it could have improved upon the network of helpers and techniques that de Jongh was largely responsible for developing and organising. The whole point was that the helpers who accompanied the evaders should blend into the environment and have quick answers to why they were accompanying men of often Anglo-Saxon appearance who could not speak French. The number of times that they brought it off is astonishing and depended more on their native wit than any training.

Soon the relations between de Jongh and her MI9 contacts in Spain became more established. The consul in Bilbao would send a message to Creswell in Madrid when he heard that de Jongh was arriving with new evaders. Creswell would then drive to Bilbao to pick up the evaders and to get an update from Dédée. He would then drive the evaders to Gibraltar via the British Embassy in Madrid.

Apart from the intelligence aspects of the operation, there were wider diplomatic considerations that Creswell had to either steer round or drive through. His boss, the British Ambassador to Madrid Sir Samuel Hoare, had his work cut out trying to prevent the Spanish dictator General Franco from following his natural fascist instincts to side with Nazi Germany. Fortunately for the Allies, Hitler and Franco did not get on. When the two leaders met at Hendaye in October 1940, despite Franco's offers of assistance to the Germans, Hitler declared that he would rather have his teeth pulled than deal with Franco.[2] However, the ideological lodestar continued to pull fascist Spain towards Berlin and it became imperative for British diplomats to make informal efforts to break this fatal attraction. The stakes were very high, for if Spain went over to the Germans, it would be almost impossible for Britain to defend Gibraltar from a landward invasion and it would lose its gateway to the Mediterranean, with all that this implied for operations in North Africa and south-eastern Europe. There would also be no chance of evaders crossing by land into Spain and getting to Portugal, which had a more friendly attitude to the British.

Letters released by MI6 reveal that Hoare sent an encrypted cable to London in June 1940 in which he spelled out what needed to be done: 'I personally urge authority be granted without delay, and that if you have doubts, the prime minister be consulted.'[3]

Hoare was referring to a plan to bribe Spanish generals and other senior officials in order to keep them onside. Churchill gave his personal consent to the initiative and millions of pounds were sent via New York to be distributed by a go-between called Juan March.[4]

In this fragile atmosphere, senior British and American diplomats were nervous about any activities that might cause the Spanish authorities to react. This included sensitivity about UK SOE or US Office of Strategic Services (OSS) operations in Spain. The same can be said of the US Ambassador Carlton J.H. Hayes. Unlike his British counterpart, Hayes enjoyed good relations with General Franco, so much so that he received some criticism, particularly from the left in the United States. However, he can be credited with keeping Franco onside and was complimented by President Roosevelt for doing so.

Portugal was also a vital escape route for refugees fleeing the German occupation of northern Europe. The Portuguese Consul-General in Bordeaux, Aristides de Sousa Mendes, helped large numbers of refugees by issuing visas that gave them safe passage. His efforts earned him a rebuke from his political masters and damaged his career. Other Portuguese consuls throughout Europe made similar efforts to help those in need.

Like Spain, Portugal was a neutral country but, unlike Spain, it had strong historic ties with England. The Treaty of Windsor of

1386 between England and Portugal is the longest-lasting mutual
support alliance between two nations in history. English merchants
had also enjoyed favourable terms in Portugal, trading commodities
that included port wine and wool. Despite having an authoritarian
unelected regime under Antonio de Oliveira Salazar, Portugal was
non-belligerent. Under the previous Republican regime, Portugal
had fought alongside the Allies in the trenches of the Western
Front in the First World War. Salazar had been sympathetic to the
Spanish nationalist cause but he was anxious that Spain should not
veer towards the Nazis. Therefore, the Portuguese Ambassador to
Madrid, Pedro Teotonio Pereira, was in a similar position to his
British and American counterparts in persuading Spain to retain
its neutral status. President Salazar was also sensitive to the plight
of the Jews and, as the Germans entered Paris in June 1940, Salazar
arranged for the office of the Hebrew Immigrant Aid Society
to be moved from Paris to Lisbon. In July 1940, the Portuguese
island of Madeira was made available for refugees from Gibraltar,
particularly women and children, as fears of an invasion of the
British possession grew. The Portuguese also made the Azores
islands available to British aircraft. This proved vital in the Battle
of the Atlantic, allowing British and later US aircraft the capa-
bility of mounting anti-submarine patrols that otherwise would
not have been possible due to the long ranges from coastal bases.
Lisbon became a spy centre with those from both the Allied and
Axis powers able to operate. On one occasion President Salazar
summoned the British Ambassador Sir Ronald Campbell after
British SOE activities organised by the SOE agent in Lisbon, John
Beevor, were deemed to be excessive and even to threaten the
Salazar regime.[5]

One of the bees in Sir Samuel Hoare's bonnet was an MI9 agent
called Donald Darling, code name Sunday. Darling had much pre-
vious knowledge of Spain, Portugal, the Basque country and the
Catalan regions of the eastern Pyrenees. SIS director Sir Claude
Dansey was quick to spot Darling's potential and he was sent to
Spain and then, after protests from Hoare, to Lisbon under the dip-
lomatic cover of 'vice-consul'. From this somewhat distant base,
Darling set about organising links for evaders to cross into Spain

from France. These included routes and safe houses to ameliorate the semi-hostile reception that they would receive from the Spanish authorities. One of Darling's key contacts was the landowner Jorge Toronja, who made available some of his extensive properties in the foothills of the Pyrenees. From these temporary lodgings evaders could then be routed via Bilbao, Barcelona and Madrid to the jump-off points for England, Lisbon and Gibraltar. Although he had good relations with the UK Ambassador to Lisbon, Sir Walford Selby, Hoare continued to resent Darling's necessarily nefarious activities and made a list of complaints against him that Darling had to face when he eventually returned to London. However, Darling had been appointed by Dansey and it was never very likely that he would be hung out to dry just because an ambassador found him an inconvenience. If Hoare was influential, Dansey was also a formidable figure who made sure that he got what he wanted. In 1944, Darling would be posted back to the Continent, this time to liberated Paris.

Escape and Evasion

The establishment of formal training in escape and evasion for British and later Allied service personnel was a significant achievement and it provides the basis of a large part of similar training in British and US armed forces today.

Major J.F.C. Holland, who had held a senior role in Military Intelligence Research, identified Norman Crockatt as a suitable person to head up the MI9 operation. Crockatt had served with distinction during the First World War as a lieutenant in the Royal Scots, winning a Distinguished Service Order (DSO) and a Military Cross (MC). He had left the army in 1927 but rejoined in 1939. Apart from his hands-on military experience on the front line, Crockatt was an efficient organiser with an aptitude for cutting through red tape. He also had the ability to forge productive relationships with relevant people, including Colin Gubbins, who was head of the SOE and who had a similarly tough, no-nonsense approach. Crockatt's brief was essentially to help British PoWs to escape. MI9 would also be trusted with collecting and distributing any information that they brought back with them. A useful side effect of helping prisoners to escape was that it caused the enemy to commit resources to preventing them. Crockatt was also aware that the enemy should not be pushed too far. The mass escape from Stalag Luft III in March 1944 and the consequent murder of about fifty Allied servicemen was a case in point. Crockatt assembled a team of hand-picked officers who would help him realise his aims, including Airey Neave, J.M. Langley, Christopher Hutton, Captain A.R. Rawlinson and Alfred John 'Johnnie' Evans. Neave, Langley and Evans all had personal experience of escaping from enemy capture. Hutton was an eccentric with a talent for devising ingenious escape devices and ways of concealing them, either in the clothing of those who might need to escape and evade or in items sent to PoW camps.

The most important element was the establishment of lectures that could be given to pilots and other personnel at high risk of capture, such as Commandos. IS9 was established in London for this purpose. As an intelligence school, its role was to train intelligence officers from all three services so that they could pass on the information to their own personnel.

One of the major effects of the training was to transform the mindset of personnel so that the prospect of being shot down and of evasion or capture was perceived as an ongoing part of military operations, demanding the same level of professional commitment as service within their active units. An event such as the downing of an aircraft and subsequent actions and events were to be seen as a continuation of their training and operations, albeit in a different context. The aim was to extinguish any sense of passive capitulation in the face of overwhelming circumstances or separation from their parent units. The United States training would go even further to explicitly say that personnel in these circumstances had been effectively transferred to a new unit. The unit in question during operations in northern Europe would be the escape line with which they came into contact. This casts a new light on the role and significance of escape lines like Comet and their leaders, such as Andrée de Jongh. These were not just freelance helpers with whom the Allied personnel might choose whether to be involved, but effectively new commanding officers whose remit would continue until those personnel were handed over to their competent US or British authorities.

The success of Allied escape and evasion operations owed much to the smooth co-operation between the British and American operations. This in turn was influenced by the people who ran those operations. On the American side, the person selected to run the US equivalent of MI9, MIS-X, was W. Stull Holt. Like Crockatt, Holt was a veteran of the Great War. In 1940 he took up the Chair of history at the University of Washington, having been recruited from Johns Hopkins University. Foreseeing the inevitability of US involvement in the war against the Axis powers, Holt rejoined USAAF in September 1941, only three months before the Japanese attack on Pearl Harbor that would bring the United States into the war. Although he was now too old for active service, Holt's transferable skills from academia were deemed appropriate for work in intelligence. In July 1942, he was summoned by Major General Carl 'Tooey' Spaatz, commanding the Eighth Air Force in England, to head up an equivalent of the British escape and evasion organisation MI9.

Fortunately for all concerned, Holt got on well with Norman Crockatt and took a pragmatic view of his brief to set up an American version of the MI9 operation. This emulated, if not replicated, the British version, leaving plenty of room for Holt to add his own ideas. As Allied air operations increased, and the number of airmen either captured or escaping and evading also increased, there was no time to be wasted and soon the British and American operations were working alongside each other and interchangeably as British and Commonwealth and American airmen received whatever help could be provided for them.

Holt's areas of responsibility included both escape and evasion and interrogation, which in turn could be divided into debriefing Allied airmen who had returned from successful bombing missions; interrogating escapers and evaders who had managed to return to base, often with the help of escape organisations such as Comet; and obtaining information from German PoWs. Holt was profoundly aware of the massive contribution made by the escape lines and resistance organisations in occupied Europe and of their courage and self-sacrifice. He made it his business to ensure that they received proper recognition once the war had ended.

There is a paucity of surviving original files on MIS-X but it is possible to work back from current doctrine on escape and evasion in USAAF to construe what was being taught to airmen in action in the 1940s. The principle of never voluntarily surrendering unless there is no other option comes across strongly in the USAAF Survival, Evasion, Resistance and Escape (SERE) manual.[6] It is also a reminder of the 'escape mindedness' that was promoted by MI9 and IS9. Even if they were captured, the SERE manual states, Isolated Personnel (IPs) must continue to resist and to make every effort to escape. It is quite clear that this is not an option to be considered but a command. Those who have not been captured are urged to spare no effort in evading the enemy and returning to an area controlled by friendly forces, employing all ingenuity and physical effort, motivated by a 'will to survive'.

The positive motivation to survive, reach friendly forces and return to the fight is accompanied by the motive to deny the enemy any advantages they may derive from the evader's capture. This includes denying the enemy any potential military information, propaganda value or use of the IP for forced labour. As stated in the IS9 lectures, the IP had to cause as much disruption to the enemy as possible by making them spend time, effort, resources and manpower in either tracking down or pursuing PoWs or evaders. Ultimately, the evader should aim to return to friendly forces armed with useful intelligence.

Under the Laws of Armed Conflict (LOAC), originating in the Geneva Conventions,[7] evaders retain their status as combatants until captured. This means that they remain under orders, whether operating on their own or in groups or under the orders of their new 'commanders', namely those who work for recognised escape organisations. They are under orders to accomplish their mission, which means returning to their own or friendly forces. As a combatant, under the LOAC, the evader is justified in attacking enemy targets and troops without fear of prosecution under criminal law.

This reminder that an evader who is part of a military force remains a combatant even though separated from their usual chain of command raises the question of how they can be identified as military combatants. The obvious answer is that they can be identified by their uniform and other identification marks. However, in order to evade successfully it is often necessary to wear some form of disguise. In occupied Europe during the Second World War, evaders were often provided with civilian clothing so that they could hide in plain sight. The SERE manual warns twenty-first-century military evaders that if they are captured while wearing a local disguise, they may expect to receive the same treatment as local civilians, unless they retain convincing legal identification such as a US armed forces ID card. Without such ID, the SERE manual warns, the captured evaders might be treated as spies, with dire immediate or long-term consequences. For evaders in northern Europe during the Second World War, the matter was further complicated by the directives issued by Hitler and the different kind of treatment to be expected by fanatical units such as the SS and Gestapo as compared with regular Wehrmacht soldiers.

On the American side, Colonel John T. Butterwick collected the anecdotes and experiences of returning evaders so that they could be used by other airmen. Butterwick was the counter-intelligence and PoW officer in the intelligence staff of General Curtis E. LeMay, who commanded the Third Air Division. He was responsible for teaching escape and evasion skills to combat air crew. In comments that reflected those of Colonel Crockatt, Butterwick stated that, ordinarily, only those who possess stamina, will and determination, together with good common sense, were able to evade the enemy and report back for duty in the United Kingdom.[8]

Apart from obvious points, such as making sure you don't lose your escape aids in the confusion of leaving an aircraft, there are other hints, such as the warning to Americans to use the word 'yes' rather than the informal 'yeah' as the latter sounded to French ears like the German '*Ja*'. They were also advised to shave regularly in order to look more like the mostly clean-shaven Frenchmen. A feature of the regular lectures were those given by successful evaders, who gave their audience the benefit of their personal experiences.

Those who attended such lectures were left in no doubt about their duty to evade capture and to return to Allied territory. The importance of taking prompt action as soon as they reached the ground was also impressed upon them. This must be seen in the context of the immediate trauma suffered by aircrew after their aircraft had been hit by flak or attacked by enemy fighters and the stress and confusion of baling out of a burning aircraft that was likely to crash or explode. Airmen were encouraged to maintain their adrenaline and sense of purpose before enemy search parties could intercept them. There was also an acknowledgement that luck often played a significant role in a successful evasion. Bumping into the right kind of people on the ground who took swift action to conceal evaders, provide them with food and put them in touch with escape organisations made a huge difference to an evader's chances.

Escape Kit

The MI9 escape kit contained a variety of essential items that were designed to provide immediate aid in emergencies, minimal sustenance and the means to fix your position, find direction and pay your way. The escape compass was often concealed in a variety of ingenious ways, including buttons, badges, fountain pens and collar studs. Maps printed on silk could be concealed in the lining of jackets. Other items included a saw blade, rubber water holder, razor, needle and thread, cash in local currencies, energy tablets, a chocolate bar and water purification tablets.

Flying boots were fitted with a pouch for a small knife that could be used to cut away the uppers of the boots and turn them into shoes.

Airmen were also warned of the dangers of parachuting to the ground, including landing in woods, which could lead to being suspended in a tree; water, with obvious dangers of drowning and being covered by the canopy; or snow, which could lead to exposure while also leaving tracks that could be followed by pursuers.

Escape and Evasion Debrief

Returning evaders provided an excellent opportunity to gather a wide range of information. This included feedback on escape equipment, the circumstances in which an aircraft was brought down, enemy tactics and ancillary information, including hearsay, that the evader might have picked up while in occupied territory. The debriefing record of Second Lieutenant Allan G. Johnston of 422 Squadron, 305 Bomb Group, is one of many examples and it provides a useful illustration of the range of information that could be gathered from successful evaders, thereby adding even more value to the work of escape organisations such as Comet and their contribution to the war effort.[9]

On 6 September 1943, Johnston was part of the crew of a B-17F Flying Fortress that flew from RAF Chelveston in Northamptonshire on a mission to bomb Stuttgart. The squadron experienced light flak while flying over France, which became more concentrated as they approached the target. On their return journey, and shortly after the rendezvous point, the engineer flagged up that they had used more than half their fuel. It became clear that other aircraft were experiencing a similar problem as some aircraft dropped from the formation and others threw out pieces of equipment to reduce weight. The problem was aggravated by a strong headwind. Johnston's aircraft descended to 8,000ft, whereupon it came under attack by several German fighters. Shells exploded in the radio room and one of the engines was damaged. They were surrounded by about fifteen enemy aircraft and eight came in for the attack from twelve, nine, six and three o'clock. These were followed by another seven fighters. The pilot had received night flying training with the RAF and used the evasive corkscrew manoeuvre, which mitigated the damage. However, the aircraft continued to take hits and, despite being wounded, the radio operator sent out an SOS. At this point the fuel ran out and the pilot gave the order to bail out. Johnston burnt the maps and made his way towards the escape hatch in the nose. He jumped out at 7,500ft and pulled the rip cord when he reached 2,000ft. A Focke-Wulf Fw 190 fighter circled him twice before tipping its wings and flying off.

As Johnson descended, he could see German soldiers on motorcycles heading towards his likely landing spot in open fields. He could see a wood nearby and he pulled on the parachute line to guide the parachute towards the wood. Before he landed, he could see German soldiers running across a field in his direction. As he entered the wood, he hit the release button and immediately ran hard in the opposite direction from the approaching soldiers. He ran up a hill and turned left at the top. He tried hiding in a bramble bush but found it did not provide enough cover, so he went on until he reached a road. He followed the road, keeping within the wood for cover. As he reached the end of the wood, he saw seven French people standing and staring at something in the distance. Johnston hid behind a tree but a boy in the group saw him and came over. He stood behind him and asked in English if he was American or English. He then called to a girl, who also came over, and they guided Johnston to a tree and told him to climb up. The tree was bushy enough to provide some protection and Johnson used his belt to strap himself to a branch. About fifteen minutes later, a German soldier with a machine gun walked past but did not look up into the tree.

After dark, the boy and girl reappeared and led Johnston for about 4km until they reached a farm. Again, they told him to climb into a tree and they returned an hour later to tell him that the coast was now clear. They showed him to a hay loft, where he stayed for three days. In due course, a man came to see him and he began his journey back to England, via Spain and Gibraltar.[10]

The initial parts of Johnston's evasion demonstrate how determination and good luck could make all the difference between evasion and capture. Even before he reached the ground, and despite being in immediate danger of capture by German soldiers who were moving to intercept him, Johnston made every effort to improve his chances by experimenting with steering the parachute into the wood. He lost no time in getting away from the pursuing soldiers before coming across the group of French people. Here good fortune intervened in the form of two children who showed remarkable ingenuity, presence of mind and maturity. Who better than a child to know which are the best trees to climb? Once he was in the relative safety of the hay loft, he was soon in the safe hands of an escape organisation.

Apart from the information he provided in his debriefing report on German fighter tactics and the usefulness of his escape kit, Johnston also gave information that he had picked up during his time with the escape organisers and resistance. This included information on tank defences, the construction of a large aerodrome, the presence of British tanks abandoned after the Dunkirk evacuation, which had been put into service with the German Army, the movement of German troops back from the Dieppe coastline, a report on the condition of a German airfield that had been bombed by the Allies and how it was now mostly used by night fighters, the presence of a large concentration camp near Toulouse, a report of SS troops firing at parachutists and the low state of morale among troops manning coastal defences. Many of these were said to be either very young or middle aged. Some German soldiers had asked Frenchmen for civilian clothes so that they could escape from military service. Although much of this was hearsay, it was nevertheless valuable to Allied military intelligence and could be cross-referenced with other reports of a similar nature.

The Net Closes

On 19/20 August 1941, the day after Dédée had left Quiévrain with Jim Cromar and the two Belgian officers, a grey Opel car with German plates turned into avenue Émile Verhaeren and proceeded slowly down the avenue as the occupants scanned the house numbers. The car stopped outside No. 73 and two men wearing civilian clothes as well as hats and leather gloves got out. One of them walked up to the door and pressed the doorbell.[1]

The men who had just arrived at Frederick de Jongh's house were members of the Geheime Staatspolizei, more commonly known as the Gestapo. From its creation in 1933 by Hermann Göring, the Gestapo had become one of the most feared state police organisations in Europe. Göring had combined a number of disparate police organisations to create the new body and in April 1934 oversight of the Gestapo was given to the head of the SS, Heinrich Himmler. By September 1939, the Gestapo was under the umbrella of the Reich Security Main Office (RSHA), alongside the security service Sicherheitsdienst (SD). In a somewhat complex series of rearrangements, the Kriminalpolizei came under the direction of the Sicherheitspolizei (SiPo). This in turn was combined with the SD to create the Reichssicherheitshauptamt, which came under the command of Reinhard Heydrich. Ultimate control of all the police forces was given to Heinrich Himmler when he assumed leadership after the assassination of Heydrich by British-trained Czechoslovak soldiers in Operation Anthropoid on 27 May 1942.

Surprisingly, despite its formidable reputation, the Gestapo was a relatively small organisation that relied heavily on networks of informants as well as leads extracted by interrogation under torture. The powers of the Gestapo were extended in such a way as to effectively place it above the law. Preventive arrest enabled the Gestapo to detain people according to the whim of its leadership. As if this was not enough, on 7 December 1941 Hitler issued the infamous Nacht und Nebel (Night and Fog) decree that ordered the imprisonment, deportation or liquidation of those considered to be enemies of the Nazi state without any documentation or right of appeal. Family and friends would have no knowledge as to the fate of the victims. The effect of this was to create a climate of fear and repression. No one knew where the fingers of this night fog would reach next. These measures were aimed in particular at the citizens of occupied territories, among whom Belgians were no exception. Those who organised or assisted escape lines were prime candidates for the Nach und Nebel treatment. Typically, Nacht und Nebel prisoners would wear special garments marked with a cross and 'NN', along with a red band. They were transported to concentration camps in overcrowded cattle wagons and once in the camps were subjected to brutal slave labour and lengthy parades. Those who fell ill or who were too exhausted to carry on could be executed on the spot. This was the potential fate that awaited enemies of the Nazi state when the Gestapo knocked on their doors.

As the bell rang, Frederick went down to open the door to the two German policemen. They asked him to confirm his identity. Once inside the house, one of the men took out a notebook and asked him if he had a daughter called Andrée. Frederick confirmed that she was his younger daughter and when they asked where she was he replied that she was in Bruges. The policeman said she was not in Bruges and asked Frederick again where she was and what she did. Frederick replied that she was a nurse and that she worked in a hospital. Apparently, the policemen looked incredulous and told Frederick that she was responsible for smuggling Englishmen as well as Belgians and that one of her accomplices had been arrested. They then asked Frederick what he did for a living and he said that he was a schoolmaster. At this point, Andrée's sister Suzanne came into the room and Frederick introduced her. The policemen asked her the same questions and she feigned innocence. After about an hour, and having taken a tour of the house, including Dédée's bedroom, the policemen left.[2]

The next day, the de Jonghs received a visit from Charles Morelle, who had travelled up from the south after his meeting with Elvire de Greef and Dédée. Morelle explained to Frederick that he was a French officer who had been sheltered by Mme Maréchal, who was English, before being escorted by Dédée over the border to France. He had a letter from Dédée for Frederick. Frederick told him that the Gestapo now knew about Dédée and her activities. Someone who worked for the clandestine newspaper *La Libre Belgique* had also informed them that Deppé had been arrested and that the authorities were looking for Dédée. Charles told him that Dédée could stay with him and his wife and sister at his house in Valenciennes and asked Frederick if he had any messages for her. Frederick asked Morelle to tell Dédée to bring him up to date with events. Morelle promised to do so.

After these eventful meetings, Frederick de Jongh continued to meet his contacts, such as Henri Michielli, who loaned him money for train tickets, food, clothing and the creation of false papers. Frederick would return to his house wondering whether his movements were being monitored. Although there was no further sign of the grey Opel or its sinister occupants, he knew that they could just be waiting until they had assembled enough information to make an arrest.

For the present, however, the work continued. He also had able and enthusiastic helpers, including Andrée Dumon (Nadine) who, since he had recruited her in October 1940, had escorted evaders to Paris, from where they could continue the journey south with the southern Comet operators, including Dédée herself. Nadine's father, Eugene Dumon, who had worked as a doctor in the Congo, was also in the resistance. His other daughter, Michelle, would be another significant player in the Comet organisation.

At the beginning of November, Frederick escorted three more RAF pilots to the Gare du Midi. They were two Polish pilots, Michel Kowalksi and Stefan Kowicki, and one Canadian, John Ives.

Frederick bought three tickets for Quiévrain and the RAF men were accompanied on the train by Elvire Morelle. Once the train reached Mons, Elvire got off and the men followed her as she got on to another train. Once they reached their destination, a young woman approached carrying a rucksack. She appeared not to notice the men but had a brief conversation with Elvire Morelle. The young woman was, of course, Andrée de Jongh.

Dédée then got on to another train and the men followed. When the train reached Lille, Dédée and the men got off. Having changed trains again, they reached Corbie, where Dédée led them to a bar. Here she addressed the men for the first time, introducing herself as Andrée de Jongh. Afterwards, it was the same routine as before. They made their way to the river Somme at dusk. They paused while a German sentry rode by on a bicycle before climbing into the boat that had been left there. When they heard a low whistle from the other side of the river, they began to make their way across and were met on the other side by Nenette. They followed her to the farm, where they were given hot soup.

The next morning, they were off again. By the evening, they were boarding a train at Austerlitz station, from where they travelled in a first-class carriage to Hendaye. When they eventually reached Bayonne, they were met by Elvire de Greef's daughter, Janine, who was accompanied by Albert Johnson, otherwise known as 'B'. They assembled in a café, where Janine ordered coffee for the group.

In due course, the evaders rendezvoused with Florentino, who gave the three men espadrilles to provide the necessary traction when climbing in the mountains. Florentino was a true countryman who knew the mountains like the back of his hand. With finely tuned senses, he was familiar with the sights and sounds of his environment and also sensitive to changes that might indicate the presence of an enemy. He had an uncanny sense of direction and otherwise unremarkable trees or stones were for him signposts.

Florentino handed round a traditional Basque gourd full of wine and then expertly caught a stream of wine that flowed into his mouth. Once they reached the top of the mountain they could see the lights of Irun and the glow emanating from Bilbao. Then they descended to the Bidassoa river, where Florentino rolled up his trousers and signalled to the others to do the same. After wading across, they then climbed up the other side until they reached a farm, where they were delighted to be served a large Spanish tortilla. While the men caught up on some sleep, de Jongh walked on alone to Renteria, where she caught a train to San Sebastián. There she contacted a helper called Santiago, who took her back to the farmhouse in his car to pick up the men. The next morning de Jongh and the men were on the early market train to Bilbao.[3]

On Christmas Day that year, 1941, Dédée appeared in Anglet accompanied by four more airmen, the Canadian Albert Day and three British airmen, Thomas Cox, Leonard Warburton and John Hutton. Day had been part of the crew of an Armstrong Whitworth Whitley medium twin-engine bomber that had taken off from RAF Topcliffe in North Yorkshire at 2207 on 5 August. They were on a mission to raid Frankfurt but had to turn back due to bad weather. The Whitley was hit by anti-aircraft fire near Coblenz and fires broke out on board. The aircraft rapidly lost height and the crew bailed out at about 5,000ft. Day landed near the village of Lochristi. It was about two o'clock in the morning. He buried his parachute and began to walk towards Ghent. As dawn broke, he kept himself hidden during the rest of the day and set off again at nightfall. He walked through the city and, although he passed some German soldiers, they ignored him, presumably because they thought his RAF uniform was one of theirs. He hid again during the next day and then set off again at night for Tielt. He asked a farmhand for food and was given food, shelter and clothing. He was then accompanied on a bicycle to Pittem, from where he walked to Lichtervelde and then to Torhout. He went to a café, where they advised him to head for Holland. However, he decided to cross a canal bridge at Leffinge, where he came across some German soldiers who were checking papers, but he kept his nerve and walked past them. On 15 August, he reached Ostend but he was unable to get on board a boat. He returned by the same route and this time swam the canal in order to avoid the soldiers. He was approached by a man in Gistel, who took him to a café, where another man took his photograph. He was then accompanied by a Belgian to Bruges, from where they caught a train to Brussels. He may not have known it at the time, but

Day was now in the hands of the Comet line. He was given an identity card and taken to a house, where he stayed for two weeks. The man he was staying with was arrested by the Gestapo and Day was taken to another house, where he met Sergeant Newton, Sergeant Bork, Sergeant Copley and Flight Lieutenant Langloise. Copley and Langloise were later captured by the Nazis. The Comet organisation provided Day with false papers but when he was due to leave with Sergeant Newton for the journey south, he was forced to remain as he had pneumonia. He then stayed in the house for another month while he recovered. On 21 December 1941, Day was taken to the station, where he met Sergeant Warburton, Sergeant Hutton and Sergeant Cox.

Warburton and Hutton had been on board a Wellington medium bomber of 101 Squadron that had taken off from RAF Oakington in Cambridgeshire at 2014 on 31 August.[4] The aircraft crashed at Boxbergheide in the western suburbs of Genk in Belgium. Three of the crew were killed and one was taken prisoner. Both Warburton and Hutton managed to parachute to the ground and evade.

It was a similar routine to previous journeys, walking up the mountainside in single file. Florentino had provided the men with espadrilles and with a stick that they would need to help them stay upright in the snow. They had been told not to speak or smoke and to go to ground as soon as either Florentino or de Jongh gave a signal.

The wind had cleared the clouds from the sky and the stars were shining bright. Although it was cold, hope seemed to shine as brightly as the stars in the dark blue canopy above them. By the time they reached the crest of the hill, however, the weather had turned. The stars were blotted out by cloud and snow began to fall. Visibility became difficult and the men were asked to put one hand on the shoulder of the person in front. They began the descent towards the river and when they had almost reached the bottom, Florentino signalled to them to wait. The message was passed back down the line, mouth to ear. It was then that they saw the Spanish frontier post. The door opened and a sentry appeared, lit by the glow of the light inside. He was holding a rifle and paused as if listening. There was only the soft sound of snow falling through the trees. Eventually the sentry turned and went back inside. Florentino then began to take off his trousers and tie them round his neck. The others did the same. Florentino waded slowly into the cold water of the river until he was up to his waist. He then turned and signalled to the first of the men to follow, holding out his hand to assist him. One by one they crossed and, having dressed again on the other side, Florentino led them through a field. They heard a truck approaching on the nearby road that led to the sentry post and de Jongh signalled to the men to hide among some pine trees. Once the coast was clear, Florentino ran across the road and signalled to the others to follow. Once they were all across, they began the long climb up the hill on the other side of the valley. They were shivering from the cold water and Day had twisted his ankle. Florentino found a sheltered area where they could rest and then passed round a gourd of Spanish cognac. Feeling revived, they set off again and in due course reached a farmhouse, where the peasant farmer lit a fire and cooked a large omelette. Later a battered old car appeared and the men climbed in. They were then taken to a rendezvous with another car. This was an English car with diplomatic number plates. The men asked de Jongh if she was coming with them. No, she replied. She needed to get back to France to pick up more airmen.[5]

Undeterred by the weather, Dédée was back on the mountains on 8 February 1942, this time accompanied by Comet helper Elvire Morelle and British airman Jackie Hogan. Once again, Florentino led them to the farm, where they were served a large tortilla before continuing on their way. The ground was covered in snow and it was slippery. Dédée heard a cry behind her. Elvire had slipped and fractured her leg and Florentino cut some branches from which to make splints to support it. It had started to rain and Florentino went off to find a mule to carry Elvire. By the time he had returned with the mule it was already daylight. Florentino then constructed a litter with more branches. It was too dangerous to move during daylight hours so they waited until nightfall. Florentino then helped Elvire on to the back of the mule and they continued to the farm. Dédée went off to find Santiago, returning in his car. They then took Elvire to San Sebastián, where a doctor was called to attend to Elvire's leg. Elvire stayed in San Sebastián until the end of March, when her brother Charlie, having escorted a British airman across the Pyrenees, accompanied her back to France.

By now the search for Comet line organisers and helpers in Belgium had intensified. Hermann Göring regarded it as a matter of personal pride that Allied airmen once shot down should not be able to find their way back to Britain where they could become operational again. If it was not the Gestapo, Comet line leaders and helpers could expect to come under the attention of the Geheime Feldpolizei (GFP).[6] This military security organisation was formed in July 1939 by Generaloberst Wilhelm Keitel and its range of duties included counter-espionage and the detection of enemy agents. In Belgium and France in particular, the GFP worked with civilian police to deter resistance activities and it was ruthless in the imposition of measures such as execution or deportation. So similar were its activities to the Gestapo that the GFP was sometimes known as the Gestapo der Wehrmacht. Groupe 530 of the GFP had been involved in the campaign in Poland before arriving in the wake of the Wehrmacht in Belgium. They were attached to Oberfeldkommandatur 672, which had rapidly been put in place after the occupation of Brussels. After a brief spell in the Cosmopolite hotel, Groupe 530 moved to No. 6 rue de la Traversière in Saint-Josse-ten-Noode. This was an imposing red brick building that had previously been the home of a religious order. From this location, the GFP set about countering resistance movements and escape lines, using whatever information that they could find, including intelligence fathered by the Abwehrstelle Belgien. Any suspects who had been imprisoned at St-Gilles would be collected by the GFP early in the morning and taken to No. 6 rue de la Traversière for interrogation. Uncooperative prisoners would be subjected to a range of torture techniques that included beatings and being forced into unnatural and painful positions for long periods. These torture techniques became more severe over time as resistance activity increased.

In 1943, the Luftwaffe were designated their own version of the GFP to distinguish it from the Wehrmacht organisation. The new organisation was called the Geheime Feldpolizei der Luftwaffe. Different sectors of the German intelligence and security community competed with each other and were effectively enemies. To some degree it might have been preferable to have been arrested by the Luftwaffe secret police rather than the Gestapo and the chances of survival might have been higher.

During February 1942, Frederick had moved to Paris, where he continued to organise the northern end of Comet operations. He then returned to Brussels to find that there was a price on his head of 1 million Belgian francs. It became clear that it was too dangerous for him to remain and on 30 April he left his home city, never to return. He would run Comet operations in Paris. Frederick's role in Brussels was briefly taken over by Henri Michieli, who was an active resistance organiser. Somewhat unwisely, Michieli organised a dinner for Charles Morelle and three intelligence agents who had been dropped by parachute. The Gestapo got wind of the meeting and arrested all of them. These arrests, along with hundreds of others, brought the Comet Brussels processing centre to a halt. Resumption of normal services would depend on Baron Jean Greindl.

The Swedish Canteen

On 10 May 1942 Baron Jean Greindl contacted Andrée de Jongh's sister, Suzanne Wittock, to ask her if there was any news of her father. Suzanne must have informed him that Frederick de Jongh had moved to Paris, upon which Greindl offered to run the Brussels end of the Comet operation. The offer was timely because, following the final departure of Frederick, the German military police had conducted wide-ranging arrests of Comet helpers in Brussels, effectively bringing the operation to a halt. Without a working network to move them on to the south, the Allied evaders would have been stuck in their safe houses for long periods of time while others were added to their number. There would have been little protection from Nazi infiltration, and they would have had no way of getting round the language barrier, no papers and no guidance. Their hosts in the various safe houses would also have been at higher risk of being discovered and then subjected to vicious interrogations in order to extract information about the network before being deported to the concentration camps. However, as so often, the Comet organisation managed to mend itself in the nick of time. Soon, Dédée arrived in Brussels for a secret meeting with Greindl, effectively giving her seal of approval to the new arrangement.

Baron Jean Greindl had been looking after family interests in the Belgian Congo, where he had built a farm, before returning to his homeland after the Belgian surrender in 1940. With a quiet manner, Greindl was an able organiser and, once given the green light by

Dédée, he set about building a network that extended well beyond Brussels. Based on Gand, Liège, Namur and Hasselt, a series of antennae using a network of personal connections would ensure that if any downed airman should arrive at a village or farm he would be quickly passed up the line until he ultimately reached Brussels, ready for despatch down the Comet line with the assistance of helpers. Greindl headed this operation from what was called the Swedish Canteen in Brussels. This was a charitable organisation set up under Red Cross auspices by the Swedish benefactor Mme Scherling. The canteen provided food and clothing for poor and sick children with packages sent from Stockholm. As director of the canteen, Greindl carried out a double role of helping both the poor children and the *enfants*, a name given to Allied evaders. Greindl lived just outside Brussels in Zellik with his wife and daughter. Not long after he took control of the operation, Dédée's sister Suzanne was arrested by the Gestapo. Greindl was helped in his administrative duties by an ex-military officer, Gaston Bidoul, and by a young woman called Peggy van Lier.[1]

Peggy, who was of South African and Irish descent, carried out a whirlwind of activities that included arranging forged papers, buying train tickets, arranging clothing and accommodation as well as recruiting suitable companions who would escort the evaders on the journey south to Paris, and who could be relied upon to step in when the men were questioned by officials in French. She had striking looks, with red hair, which was entirely consistent with her vivacious personality.

Greindl, known by his code name 'Nemo', created not so much a network as a web of connections throughout Belgium that was acutely sensitive to any contact by Allied airmen seeking refuge. Typically, once a contact had been made, for example with a local farmer, the local priest, doctor or other official would be advised. The likelihood was that any one of these would know who the local Comet line contact was and the information would be passed on. The Comet line centres created by Greindl covered the main Belgian regions of Flanders, the Ardennes and Limbourg. However, the system was not designed to just passively wait for contacts. Greindl listened for any news of an Allied aircraft being shot down and would then arrange for a Comet agent to be despatched to the area to make inquiries. This increased the likelihood of Allied airmen falling into the right hands and minimised the danger of being betrayed by an informer. It was a matter of spreading the word by contacting reliable people so that the inquiries gradually branched out. If all went well, a reply would eventually come back down the grapevine with details of where the airmen were being held. The danger was ever-present that someone in the network could be a turncoat in the pay of the Nazis, placing both the pilots and the Comet agent in danger of interception and capture. Comet agents would carry out a reconnaissance of the area to assess the potential dangers and to decide how quickly the airmen should be taken up the line. There was also a danger that the airman himself might be a plant by the Germans to draw in Comet line agents and blow their network. By 1942, the Germans made fewer attempts to plant airmen and instead focused on turncoat guides for the escape lines.[2]

An example of how quickly and efficiently the Comet network could work was the downing of RAF Armstrong Whitley V BD344 on 31 July 1942. The twin-engine heavy bomber of 24 Operational Training Unit (OTU) had taken off from RAF Honeybourne in Worcestershire at 2340 hours the previous evening bound for Düsseldorf.[3] The Whitley was powered by two Rolls-Royce X engines. It had a single machine gun at the front and four .303 machine guns at the rear. It was becoming obsolete by 1942 but, despite its rather plodding manner, the workhorse was generally popular with crews. The crew of BD344 were pilot officer Geoffrey Silva (Royal Australian Air Force) of New South Wales, Sergeant J.B. Black, Sergeant W.T. Whiting and Sergeant A.J. Whitcher. As the aircraft approached its objective, it was hit by enemy flak. The wireless operator, Whiting, was wounded and the tail gun unit was damaged. However, the Whitley flew on and dropped its bomb load on the target before turning back for home. Lumbering in the summer night sky and with few defences, the Whitley was vulnerable and soon it was under attack from one if not more Luftwaffe night fighters. With the aircraft ablaze, the crew started to bail out. Silva and Whicher parachuted within reasonable proximity of each other, but Whicher was wounded when he hit the ground. The plane crashed near Fleurus in Wallonia, south of Brussels. Silva carried Whicher to a nearby farm. The farmer called a doctor, who appeared with two bicycles. He treated Whicher's injury and the farmer provided food and a place to sleep. The next morning, the two were on the way north to Brussels, where they were met by Peggy van Lier. She organised the necessary false papers and train tickets and escorted them to the station. Soon they had arrived in Paris, where they were met by another Comet helper and shown to a flat in the rue Oudinot. There they met Frederick and Andrée de Jongh. The next day Dédée accompanied them to the Gare Austerlitz and on to a train bound for Bayonne. Dédée and Florentino then accompanied the two airmen over the Pyrenees and to San Sebastián, where they were picked up by a British Embassy car. Next stop Gibraltar.

Geoffrey Silva would later be commended for his courage and fortitude in pressing home the attack on Düsseldorf despite the damage to his aircraft. He later transferred to 210 Squadron RAF Coastal Command and lost his life on 13 June 1943 with the nine other crew members of a Consolidate PBY Catalina in the Bay of Biscay. The Comet line could get people home, but it could not guarantee their survival for the rest of the war.

The delicate tightrope walk that Jean Greindl had to negotiate was highlighted on one occasion by a visit by the benefactress Mme Scherling, accompanied by none other than the Militärbefehlshaber Baron von Falkenhausen. Baron Alexander Ernst Alfred Hermann Freiherr von Falkenhausen had been appointed military governor of Belgium in May 1940. His uncle, Baron Ludwig von Falkenhausen, had served in the same role in Brussels during the First World War and the Edith Cavell incident. Alexander was by nature a moderate and was opposed to the more extreme elements of the Nazi party. Nevertheless, he succumbed to pressure from the RSHA under Heydrich and about 28,900 Jews were deported under his watch, many to work on the coastal defences known as the Atlantic Wall. One of the defining moments of Falkenhausen's administration was the explosion of a bomb outside the Gestapo headquarters in avenue Louise in December 1941. This coincided with the sabotage of some electricity pylons. German high command demanded that Falkenhausen should execute random hostages as a reprisal.

Falkenhausen decided to take a more moderate route and instead ordered the execution of three resistance fighters who had already been condemned to death a month earlier but who might have been eligible for a reprieve. Measures became more repressive after the order of enforced labour in Germany on 6 October 1942. The Militärverwaltung headed by Falkenhausen had relatively few staff and depended largely on maintaining existing civil structures with German oversight. The Militärveitlungstaab looked after political, socio-economic and cultural affairs and was headed by Falkenhausen's deputy, Eggert Reeder. Falkenhausen was seen to be an ally of the anti-Hitler plotters and after the assassination attempt on Hitler on 20 July 1942 he was removed from office and then arrested. He was sent to various concentration camps culminating in Dachau, where he was captured by the US 5th Army when they relieved the camp. He was tried in Belgium in 1951 and sentenced to three years' hard labour, though his sentence was curtailed and he received a pardon from Chancellor Konrad Adenauer.

Falkenhausen had come to inspect the good works at the Swedish Canteen and was introduced to Greindl, who was understandably somewhat taciturn in the presence of the German field marshal and his aide-de-camp. It so happened that on that very day Greindl had also hosted a captain in the RAF who was en route to the south.

The pressure on the Comet line continued. On 11 August 1942, the GFP arrived at the Dumon house early in the morning. Eugene Dumon and his daughter Andrée (Nadine) attempted to escape but the house was surrounded. Eugene and Nadine were taken separately to the rue de la Traversière, where Nadine was put in solitary confinement prior to interrogation accompanied by beatings and threats of execution. In September 1942 she was sent to St-Gilles prison. A year later, she would be designated Nacht und Nebel and deported to the concentration camps. She would endure both Ravensbrück and Mauthausen before being relieved by the Red Cross in April 1945. Eugene died at Gross-Rosen concentration camp on 9 February 1945.

Meanwhile, Allied bombers continued to be brought down by flak or night fighters. Flight Lieutenant Leonard Charles Pipkin was the navigator in a Halifax II W1219 of RAF 103 Squadron that took off from RAF Elsham Wolds on 6 September 1942 bound for a raid on Duisburg at the centre of the Rhine–Ruhr region.[4] The Halifax appears to have been shot down by a night fighter of 3./NJG1 at 4 a.m. It crashed at Tegelen, 5km south-west of Venlo in the Netherlands. The rear gunner, Sergeant Charles Edward Banstead, was killed. Five other crew members were captured and taken prisoner, while Pipkin alone managed to evade.[5]

When Pipkin reached the ground, he was fortunate that there was so much confusion as a result of the bombing that he was not immediately noticed. He was spotted, however, when walking into a wood but he managed to keep out of sight by covering himself in leaves while soldiers combed the area. Later, while walking along a road, he was accosted by an unarmed German soldier, who tried to arrest him. After a struggle that ended with the two men rolling into a ditch full of water, Pipkin walked away free, leaving the dead German behind him. Pipkin then crossed the river Niers into the Netherlands and came to a farmhouse, where he was given board and lodging. In due course, a priest appeared and reassured him that he was in safe hands. On 11 September, a guide took him across a river, where they came across two men with bicycles. He was accompanied to another farmhouse, where he was told that an organisation would take him over the border into Belgium. This, of course, was the Comet line and, in due course, Pipkin was accompanied over the Pyrenees before travelling with British diplomats to Gibraltar.[6]

At 1828 on 24 October 1942, Halifax II W1188 'D' for Donald of 103 Squadron, RAF, again took off from RAF Elsham Wolds.[7] Among the crew of eight, which included a reserve pilot due to there being a long leg to Milan and back, was Warrant Officer Herbert J. 'Dizzy' Spiller. Having donned his Sidcot flying suit, Herbert boarded the aircraft and settled himself in behind his navigator's table. He checked his wrist chronometer and set about his immediate preparation routine, which started with sharpening pencils. There was a good reason for this. If the aircraft was attacked and had to change course, he would need to plot an alternative course rapidly. This was to be the squadron's last operation flying Halifax bombers as they were soon to be re-equipped with the Avro Lancaster.

Once the pilot, Squadron Leader Sidney Fox, had done his final engine checks and received a signal from an Aldis Lamp, they began to move around the perimeter of the airfield until they reached the end of the runway. A green light indicated that they were cleared for take-off and soon they were powering down the runway and lifting into the evening sky.

Once they had passed Cambridge and then the Isle of Sheppey, they headed over the dark waters of the Channel until they were greeted with light flak as they came over the French coast. All the crew were on edge, though none gave it away in their behaviour or tone of voice, least of all the captain, who asked them to keep an eye out for night fighters. The large aircraft with its powerful engines nevertheless induced a sense of security that was immediately shattered when a bullet ricocheted off the steel panel that separated Herbert's position from the wireless operator. The Halifax veered over to its port side and the captain announced that both the port engines and wing were on fire. It was not long before the captain ordered the crew to abandon the aircraft immediately. Amid the noise and confusion, Herbert somehow managed to put his parachute on the wrong way up and he then had to remove it and turn it the right way. Then the exit hatch jammed until it was eventually kicked open. The crew all remembered their training and took it in turns to jump in the right order. Soon Herbert was floating in silence as his parachute opened above him.

Herbert Spiller's experience of coming under attack unexpectedly was all too familiar to RAF bomber crews. Flak was at least visible to aircrew, and audible if close enough, but there was little to prepare them for the silent attack of a night fighter. The German night fighter division was commanded by Josef Kammhuber, who had a background in co-ordinating flak, searchlight and radar units. The division was divided into several wings, the most successful of which was Nachtjagdgeschwader 1 (NJG 1). In July 1940, the headquarters of the Night Fighter Division was moved to Brussels. The Germans developed an early-warning radar system called Freya to detect British bombers as they approached. This was later supplemented by a short-range radar system call Würzburg. The Luftwaffe night fighters were fitted with their own radar systems so that they could lock on to an individual bomber and make their approach. Kammhuber also developed tactics for the night fighter pilots whereby they would approach an unsuspecting bomber from behind and below, rather like a sniper approaching its target, and out of sight of the bomber's rear gunner. The night fighter would then get as close as within 50 yards of the bomber and then pull up on its tail before firing its powerful cannon, the forward movement of the bomber meaning that it was raked from front to rear with shells.[8]

Herbert landed in a wood and was knocked out by the fall when he released himself from the parachute that had left him dangling in a tree. Having also lost a boot in the fall, once he regained consciousness he had to stagger about until he could bind some material around his foot. Boosted by a couple of caffeine tablets from his escape kit, he managed to make his way to a house in the small village of Ligny-en-Barrois, where a young couple with children took him in. They gave him soup, bread and cheese, and treated his wounds. They also helped him to verify where he was on his silk map. Aware of the danger that he was putting the family in by his presence, Herbert then moved on until he found a shed where he spent the night. The next day he walked towards Bar-le-Duc, passing German patrols on the way, who did not pay him any attention. He then moved on to St-Dizier, where he approached a priest in a Catholic church and he introduced him to the abbot. They told him that he should go to Paris, where he could find help. Once he arrived in the capital, he went to another Catholic church where the abbot gave him food and put him in touch with the local resistance. After being interrogated by two burly men to check that he was not a Nazi plant, he was accompanied by a woman in her thirties to her parents' flat.

Herbert was taken on a somewhat roundabout route via Holland, back to France, and then to Brussels. A sequence of young women guided him and play acted as his girlfriend, an arrangement with which Herbert was more than happy to comply. He met a Canadian called Smitty from the Royal Canadian Air Force (RCAF) in a safe house and they waited to meet the guide who would take them south. They were shown into a room where they saw a young, vibrant woman who was evidently completely in command of the situation and who lost no time in briefing them about what was to happen next. This, of course, was Andrée de Jongh and, having checked their papers and issued them with train tickets to Bayonne, she briefed them on the Comet line protocols about how to behave when they were out and about. When she accompanied them to the station, they acted as if they were separate individuals, though they always kept Dédée within sight. Having passed through the barriers without incident, they boarded the same carriage and sat apart. Once they arrived at Bayonne, de Jongh took them to a café, where they met 'B' Johnson. They then took a bus to Anglet, from where they could see the mountains in the distance as well as the blue sea. They were given lunch by Elvire de Greef at her villa, where Herbert noted the name of his gunner friend Jack Newton from 12 Squadron in the 'visitors' book'. They then caught the train to St-Jean-de-Luz. On arrival, they picked up bicycles that had been left for them and then set off for the foothills of the Pyrenees where they would meet their mountain guide. Once they had reached the village of Urrugne, they left their bicycles and set off up a cart track that led to Francia Usandizaga's house. In the company of Francia and her two young children, they were given a meal. Florentino arrived dressed in a dark blue smock and linen trousers. His huge size made an impression on the men and he issued them with goatskin botas to carry liquid refreshment, espadrilles and sturdy walking sticks.[9]

Once Florentino was satisfied that their espadrilles were tied tightly, the party set off, consisting of Herbert and his fellow airman Smitty, a doctor and five young Frenchmen, with Florentino leading and de Jongh bringing up the rear. Soon soft grass gave way to slippery stones and they were glad of their sticks to keep their balance. After a while, a message was passed down the line to stop, each person putting their hand behind them as a signal. Comet methods were as well worked out as military drills. After a quick conversation with Florentino, Dédée drew them into a semicircle to tell them that they must make extra efforts to keep quiet as this was a heavily patrolled area. After they had moved on for a while, there was an even more urgent command to get down, upon which they all fell on their faces. It did not take long to discern the reason as they heard voices carried through the cold mountain air. When the immediate danger passed, they moved on again with even greater haste in order to get out of the danger area. When they reached the summit, they could see the flickering lights of Irun, the flash of the lighthouse at Fuenterabbía and in the distance the glow of San Sebastián.

The descent proved even more painful than the ascent, but rocks eventually gave way to softer ground and now they could hear the distant roar of the river below. There was still plenty of reason for caution as bumping into Spanish Guardias Civiles could mean imprisonment in a Spanish concentration camp or return to France to face the Gestapo. Eventually they reached the riverbank, where they were instructed by Dédée and Florentino on the procedures for crossing the river. This included removing their trousers and tying them around their necks so that the person behind could hold on to a free trouser leg. There was a Spanish border post nearby and the ever-present danger that a searchlight would probe the night as they kept a watch for smugglers. Florentino tied a rope to a tree on the bank and then waded out, stopping in the middle of the river and signalling the others to follow. When they reached him, he let go of the rope and they continued, holding on to each other and fighting to retain their footing against the current. There was an order to get down close to the water as the searchlight flashed and then illuminated the bank that they had just left. When it moved on, they continued until they reached shallower water and made their way onto the opposite bank.

While they all sighed with relief after the dangerous river crossing, and began to put their trousers back on, de Jongh informed them of two further obstacles up ahead. First was the railway line and beyond that a road. They scrambled up the bank and waited for Florentino's signal before running across the railway line. Then they scrambled up another bank until they reached the road to Irun. This would be more tricky as traffic was intermittent and there was a guard post further down the road. One by one, they moved up to crouch next to Florentino until he gave the signal. Then they dashed across the road and hid themselves in the undergrowth beyond. Once they were all safely across, the journey continued. They marvelled as they saw the Peñas de Aya, or mountain with three crowns, and in due course they were descending to green meadows and a welcoming farmhouse where, true to Comet organisation, they received a warm welcome and Spanish omelettes.[10]

Then came the time to part. Dédée informed Herbert and Smitty that a car was waiting for them on the road outside. The rest would go on their separate journeys. They bid farewell to those who had shared the common bond of danger in the quest for freedom and then went out with de Jongh towards the car. It had a diplomatic number plate and they were greeted by a well-spoken young Englishman. When they thanked de Jongh for all that she had done, they asked her if she was planning to stay long. No, she said. She was going back to France that night.

Apart from Peggy van Lier, there was another significant appointment made by Jean Greindl during his tenure at the Swedish Canteen. This person would revitalise the Comet line in the south, first in association with Andrée de Jongh and then, after her capture by the Nazis, largely on his own. His name was Jean-François Nothomb, later given the tongue-in-cheek code name of Franco. With his thick black hair and square jaw Franco could pass unnoticed as an ordinary Belgian citizen. He had a strong religious faith and would invariably gravitate towards the nearest Catholic church during his travels. After the Belgian surrender in 1940, Nothomb, who had been serving in the Belgian Army, had been sent off to Germany with other PoWs. He was first put in a work gang and then sent to Stalag IX-C near Leipzig. His first escape attempt failed but, about six months after his arrival at the camp, he managed to escape on his second attempt and caught a train to Luxembourg. He settled there for a while, having obtained false papers that convinced the relevant authorities. He then took a job working with children in the Cistercian monastery of Abbaye Notre-Dame d'Orval in the Gaume region of Belgium. He came into contact with Comet helper Victor Michiels and told him about his plans to move to England, where he planned to join the free Belgian forces and continue the fight against the Nazis. Victor told Nothomb about the work of the Comet line and that he would serve his country better by helping Allied airmen return to Britain. Michiels arranged an introduction to Jean Greindl in Brussels and Jean-François was impressed by the calm but decisive manner of the Comet leader. For his part, Greindl recognised that Nothomb might be the perfect person to fulfil Andrée de Jongh's request for an associate for the southern Comet operations. Dédée must have guessed that her luck might run out and that she would need to hand over to someone whom she could rely on to continue the work. Greindl therefore suggested to Nothomb that he should get on a train to Paris, where he would meet Dédée. Nothomb agreed and, having arrived in Paris, was directed to the flat in rue Oudinot that Frederick de Jongh was using as his HQ for Paris operations and transits. Nothomb was greeted by both Frederick and Elvire Morelle. Frederick was pleasant but reserved, whereas Elvire was forthcoming and welcoming. When he was shown to his room he looked out of the window where he could see the crucifix atop the church of Les Invalides. It spoke to him of both hope and pain. At the first opportunity, he went out to attend Mass at the church of St Francis Xavier. When he returned, he found that Dédée had arrived, having travelled all night from the Spanish border.[11]

Fortunately for them both, the chemistry was right. Dédée appreciated Nothomb's straightforward manner and he felt instantly at ease in her company. Once they had discussed his role as a guide, Elvire suggested the code name Franco, with a nod to the Spanish dictator. The interview stage over, Frederick and Dédée produced false papers and tickets for the four airmen, two British and two Russians, whom they would be accompanying to the south. Having rendezvoused with the men, they boarded an express train to Hendaye that left the Gare Austerlitz at 9.30 a.m. When the train reached Bayonne, Elvire de Greef boarded and accompanied the group to St-Jean-de-Luz. It was Sunday and, soon after arrival, Nothomb made his way to the church in the town to attend Mass. Afterwards he went for a swim in the Atlantic, pleased to discover that the water was still relatively warm for October. When evening came, and in order not to attract attention to themselves, they began to move in small groups up the hill towards Francia's house and there awaited the arrival of Florentino.

Once Florentino had arrived, and while Francia produced a bowl of milk, he went through the usual practical preparations of issuing espadrilles to each of the evaders. Once they were all ready, Florentino led the way up the mountain with de Jongh behind him, the men in Indian file behind her and Nothomb bringing up the rear. They walked for eight hours with barely a break until they got to a ruined farmhouse. By four o'clock in the morning they had reached

Oyarzun, where they came upon a small auberge. Florentino threw stones at the window to wake the owner and once he had opened his door to them he set about preparing a substantial tortilla. By now, they were all ravenous.

Both Dédée and Nothomb had brought with them a change of clothing and, having changed, they both set off at about 5 a.m. After walking only about 100m, they came upon a car. Dédée spoke to the chauffeur and in due course the four evaders were taken off in the car while Dédée and Nothomb continued on foot to Renteria, where they caught a train to San Sebastián and stayed there for four days. The four evaders had been taken to a rendezvous with a British diplomatic car and were soon on their way to Madrid.[12]

The time in San Sebastián gave Dédée and Nothomb an opportunity to recuperate and also for her to explain to him some of the tricks of the trade, including her recommendation that he should always choose to travel in a first-class compartment with evaders. There were only six places available in such a compartment, which reduced the possibility of others being in there and creating language difficulties if anyone should ask a question or wish to make conversation. There were also less rigid controls for first class.

This brief interlude in the south would prove vital for the future of the Comet line but dark clouds were now gathering over Brussels.

The Trap

Considering the challenges he faced, Jean Greindl's organisational efforts along with those of his dedicated staff and helpers, including Peggy van Lier, had achieved considerable success. Without his countrywide network, evading airmen might well have had to fend for themselves, sharply reducing their chances of escape. Apart from routing the evaders through Brussels and on to trains to Paris where they could be picked up by the Paris and southern networks of the Comet line, he had also introduced a key organiser in the form of Nothomb. However, the German authorities were also acutely aware that Allied aircraft crews who had parachuted from damaged aircraft were disappearing as if into thin air. They were relentless therefore in their efforts to track down the people and the organisations that were helping them to escape.

Although somewhat clumsy in its execution, the targeting of the Maréchal household by the Gestapo in November was a major blow to the Comet organisation in Brussels and brought the Germans one step closer to Greindl's nerve centre at the Swedish Canteen.

The Abwehr was based in Brussels at No. 6 rue de la Traversière, where it could compare notes with its fellow occupants, the Geheime Feldpolizei (GFP). The Abwehr was the intelligence organisation for the Wehrmacht and came under the Oberkommando der Wehrmacht, which reported directly to Hitler. The Abwehr itself was commanded by Admiral William Canaris. The Abwehr and Canaris were at odds with the SS and SD under Reinhard Heydrich, who was critical of the poor performance of German military intelligence during the First World War. Group III of the Abwehr was responsible for countering resistance organisations and their activities. Abwehr agents were infiltrated into resistance groups, leading to arrests and interrogations, often under torture.

Although MI9 in London had warned about likely attempts by German military intelligence to infiltrate the organisation, the measures that were taken by the Comet line were somewhat elementary and easy for a professional intelligence organisation such as the Abwehr to get around. These included a list of questions to evaders to check their bona fides, such as which air base they had flown from and the type of aircraft they had flown in. However, it is one thing to ask questions and another to know what action to take if the answers sounded improbable. These, after all, were just ordinary people who nevertheless showed extraordinary pluck, presence of mind and fortitude.

The Maréchal family in avenue Voltaire were among the most effective supporters of the Comet line. Georges Maréchal and his English wife, Elsie, were also admirers of Edith Cavell and her witnesses during the First World War. Early photographs of Elsie show an English rose but, as events would reveal, this rose was equal to all that a Nazi winter could throw at it, and the same could be said for her daughter and namesake. Georges Maréchal had spent some time recuperating in England during the First World War when he met Elsie Mary Bell, who was then working as a teacher. They married and, having spent some time in Germany where Georges was working, they had three children, the first of whom died when young, as well as Elsie and Robert.

Georges was a member of the clandestine Belgian intelligence-gathering organisation Luc, which became active in September 1940.[1] It was soon sending regular intelligence updates to London and was praised by Winston Churchill after the war. Luc was particularly successful in gathering information about German radar installations and managed to obtain a map of German night fighter control systems in western Belgium. This was vital intelligence in light of the threat posed to Allied bombers by Luftwaffe night fighters. Georges was also a member of the conservative paramilitary

organisation Les Trois Mousquetaires (LTM), which was primed
for action on the return of Allied forces. Despite its conservative origins, LTM later collaborated with the left-wing Front
d'Independence and together they would play a significant role
during the liberation of Belgium. Strangely enough, the German
authorities never came to know about Georges' resistance activities; he was arrested and tried due to his association with the work
for the Comet line largely performed by his wife and daughter in
sheltering and aiding evaders. Such activities were liable to the
most severe punishments, including interrogation under torture,
trial by a military court, execution or deportation to a concentration camp. Visitors to the Maréchal house had included Andrée de
Jongh, the French officer Charles Morelle, who was so impressed
by the Comet organisation that he decided to join it and offered his
house in Valenciennes as an alternative base for Comet operations,
and his sister Elvire. Another long-term lodger had been Pierre
Courtois, a schoolmaster at Robert Maréchal's school who had
been betrayed by Prosper Dezitter. Due to a clerical error, Courtois
was released from St-Gilles prison and in due course found his way
to England.

The 18-year-old Elsie performed a valuable role for Comet as
she was bilingual and could therefore talk to English-speaking
airmen and check their details. Looking somewhat younger than
her age, she would move around Brussels and outlying areas while
attracting little suspicion from the German authorities. She was
much valued by Jean Greindl and young Elsie found him to be a
courteous and considerate leader. Young Elsie busied herself with
finding everyday essentials that the evaders would need for their
onward journey through France, including clothes and food as
well as photographs for false papers. She would also take trips into
the surrounding countryside to collect evaders from villages and
farms and to accompany them back into the city. She would liaise
with trusted members of local communities, who would advise the
Comet network of any Allied evaders in their area. Young Elsie
was taught many of her skills by Peggy van Lier, who like her was
bilingual in French and English. Airmen would occasionally stay
at the Maréchal home and the two women enjoyed their company.

To them, the young airmen were a source of hope amid the dark clouds of Nazi occupation. It goes without saying that the British, Commonwealth and American airmen were cheered to be looked after by people who spoke their own language. One of these visitors was Flying Officer Ivan Davies of the Royal Australian Air Force (RAAF).

Davies was the navigator in Halifax II W7750 'NP-M' of 158 Squadron that had set off from RAF East Moor in North Yorkshire at 0029 on 7 August 1942 bound for a raid on Duisburg.[2] Situated at the entrance to the Ruhr industrial region, Duisburg was a major target for the RAF as it was a site of significant steel, iron and chemical industries. Halifax W7750 was one of 215 aircraft on the raid and one of five that were lost. Their route should have taken them over Holland but the aircraft was off course and flying to the south. Flight Officer Davies worked out a new course setting to get them back on track and Flight Lieutenant Jeffrey Haydon pulled on the controls to take them north. As he did so, there was a loud impact as machine gun shells ripped into the fuselage. Flames shot through the aircraft and the incendiary bombs on board started to burn. Haydon threw the Halifax into a dive in an attempt to put out the fire and evade their assailant. He also ordered the bombs to be released but they could not reach the release mechanism due to the flames. Haydon then ordered the crew to prepare to jump, starting with the rear gunner, Sergeant Gray. However, Gray was compromised by the flames and could not reach his parachute. The front escape hatch was opened and both Flight Officer Davies and Sergeant Huddless jumped first. Huddless' parachute failed to open and he was killed in the fall. While Haydon fought to control the aircraft, the other crew members jumped, with Haydon leaving last. The aircraft later exploded and crashed between the villages of Opglabbeek and Gruitrode.

The crew parachuted fairly close to each other and landed near the village of Maaseik. Haydon landed in a pine forest and immediately covered his parachute with branches. He headed north and after about 5 miles he came across a 14-year-old boy, who led him to his parents' farm at Maaseik. He stayed there for two days, glad of the opportunity to rest his leg, which he had hurt in the jump. His hosts contacted two brothers in Maaseik and he was taken to their house, where he stayed for another three days. He was then moved to Dilson, where he stayed with a woman before being escorted to Liège.

Sergeant Fox landed in the same wood as Haydon and walked about 5 miles before he came to a farm, where he was sheltered. He was assisted by a Catholic priest and hidden in a wood where two boys brought him clothes and a bicycle. They cycled to Dilsen, where he stayed in a house near a windmill. Sergeant Fox then moved on to Liège, where he met Haydon. Meanwhile, Flight Officer Ivan Davies made his way west and followed a railway line leading towards Genk. He reached the Albert Canal and found his way to a farm, where the farmer told him that he would make arrangements with a relative who had connections with the escape lines.

In this business of collecting evaders, the GFP were often not far behind. On one occasion, young Elsie went to the village of Blauwberg, 30 miles north-east of Brussels, to collect Earl Price, a Canadian airman who had been hiding in a wood and who was then taken to a boarding house run by a Madame Delogie. Only thirty minutes after young Elsie and Price left the boarding house, the GFP arrived on the scene and arrested Madame Delogie.

The growing numbers of evaders coming into the system prompted Greindl to make changes to the way the collections were organised. Instead of sending helpers such as young Elsie to meet the evaders, he arranged for guides to bring them into the city. Advance notice of their arrival was by a system of postcards sent to a shop run by the Deceunynck family. The message would read, 'Packet to collect at the usual place at [a certain time] on [a certain date].' The daughter of the family, Nelly, sometimes delivered the postcards to the Maréchal home or young Elsie would go around to the shop to collect them. The 'usual place' referred to St Joseph's church in Orban square, which was within easy reach of the Luxembourg station where the guides and evaders usually arrived. The meeting would take place inside the church at the confessional of Fr Costenoble, whose reputation was such that there were usually several people waiting for confession. This enabled the new arrivals to blend in without drawing attention to themselves. Code phrases would be exchanged between the Comet helper and the guide, after which young Elsie or another Comet member would go outside and sit on a bench, followed in due course by the guide and evaders. Here the Comet member would run through verification checks with each evader, which typically included questions about their name, rank and number, the type of aircraft they had flown in and where it had crashed, how many crew were on board as well as random questions about things that the average Allied airman might be expected to know. These questions had been suggested by MI9 in London after the Germans had tried to infiltrate agents disguised as airmen. Once she was satisfied, young Elsie – sometimes helped by Nelly – would then escort the men either to her own house or to another safe house. As the threat from the GFP and Gestapo grew, Greindl decided to stop using the Maréchal home as a safe house.[3]

The Maréchal family were close to the de Jongh family and they collaborated with the intention and organisation of the Comet line from the beginning. Elsie Mary played a valuable role in recruiting lodgers and other helpers for the Comet line in Belgium in support of the revised Comet organisation under Greindl.

On 19 November 1942, however, things did not appear to be going to plan. A green envelope was pushed through the letter box of the Maréchal home. Mrs Maréchal showed it to her daughter and asked her if she knew anything about it. Elsie opened the envelope and pulled out the note inside, which read: '*Deux [colis] pour jeudi.*' Elsie was concerned as, apart from the cryptic nature of the note, it broke their standard procedures for a note to be delivered directly to the house. Usually, advance warnings were sent on a postcard and they were normally sent two or three days in advance of the arrival of the guide and evaders. With typical presence of mind, Elsie told her mother that she was going to share her concerns with Greindl. She took a tram to the rue Ducale but when she arrived at the Swedish Canteen he was not there.[4]

Meanwhile, Comet helper 26-year-old Albert Marchal crossed the Frère-Orban square accompanied by two men. He went into the church of St Joseph but found that there was no escort waiting for him there as usually arranged. Albert waited for fifteen minutes until the church clock sounded twelve o'clock. When no one appeared, Albert decided to take the men to Nelly's house. Nelly was not in and her parents directed Albert to the Maréchals' house. By now Elsie had returned from the Swedish Canteen. She and her mother had seen Albert and the two men approaching from a window and when there was a knock at the door, despite their concerns about this direct approach to the house, contrary to the agreed procedures, Elsie opened the door. Albert explained that there had been no one at the arranged meeting point and that Nelly had told him that the only safe house she knew of was the Maréchal house. He told them that he planned to return to Namur. Mrs Maréchal and Elsie showed the men to the sitting room, where Elsie remarked on their unusual accents. The men explained that they were Americans serving with the RAF. Elsie said that they were the first Americans that they had met.[5]

The behaviour of the men was unusual. When offered food, they said that they were not hungry. Allied airmen who had been passed through the Comet network after being shot down invariably had hearty appetites. Their excuse was that they had drunk too much whisky the night before. This was also strange since whisky was almost impossible to get hold of in occupied Belgium. After more awkward exchanges, Elsie showed them to the sitting room and handed them each a piece of paper. She asked them to write down their names, their RAF numbers, the call sign of their aircraft and details of the place where they had landed. The men glanced at each other and asked if this was necessary. Elsie assured them that this was an indispensable part of their routine checks. She noted that this was the first time that she had been challenged by evaders about this. Once the men had filled out the questionnaire, Elsie took back the papers.

She asked one of the men to confirm that their aircraft was a Halifax.

'Yes,' replied the man.

'How many of you were there in the aircraft?' asked Elsie.

'Four,' answered the man. 'I don't know what happened to the other two.'

'Only four?' said Elsie with surprise. 'That's rather a small number for such a large aircraft.'

She was right. The Halifax was a four-engine heavy bomber with a minimum crew of seven. German bombers typically had a crew of four or five.

At this point one of the men stood up and announced that they would like to get some fresh air. Elsie replied that they were free to go into the garden. The man said that they would rather go for a longer walk outside. Elsie and her mother were surprised as evaders did not usually want to go out into the streets of an occupied country for obvious reasons. For their part, the German agents had probably realised by now that they were under suspicion, not having reckoned on meeting fluent English speakers. It was time to call in reinforcements.[6]

Once the men had left, Elsie turned to her mother and expressed her concerns. The men neither looked like nor behaved like any RAF pilots that she had come across before. She told her mother that she planned to go to the Swedish Canteen to discuss the situation with Greindl. As she left the house and walked down the street, she turned to check if she was being followed. It also occurred to her that the RAF pilots she had met wore blue shirts, whereas these two men were wearing khaki shirts. Once she reached the Swedish Canteen and walked into Greindl's office, she could tell from his expression and that of his assistant Bidoul that something was wrong. They had received news of arrests of Comet members in Liège by the Gestapo.

Elsie told them about the two new evaders who had come from Namur and who had arrived at her house accompanied by Albert. Jean expressed surprise that he had not been informed. Elsie showed him the green note that had come through the letter box. Having read it, Jean asked why the men had gone directly to the house. Elsie replied that she did not know, which was why she was there. Jean asked whether the handover had taken place at St Joseph's church. He was astonished to hear that Albert had not found anyone waiting for the handover and that he had then gone to Nelly's house, from where he had been directed to the Maréchal house.

First Liège and now this. Jean put his head in his hands. The system he had set up with such care seemed to be crumbling around him. Elsie was close to tears and Jean tried to reassure her. He asked to see the note again. He pointed out to Bidoul that the letter 'a' was written in the German style. Then he asked Elsie to return to the house and get as much information as she could before reporting back.

For all his laudable organisational achievements in setting up a successful network for evaders in Belgium throughout the regions as well as the shelter and transfer of evaders through Brussels to the south, this was Greindl's moment of truth and tragically he failed to see what should already have been apparent. The Comet network had been blown and he did not need Elsie to return to her house to provide him with more evidence of what was staring him in the face. Unfortunately, it would not be his first mistake that day. Elsie set off for home, hoping that she would get back before the two men had returned from their walk.

Meanwhile, back at the house, the men had already returned. Mrs Maréchal tried to make conversation until suddenly the doorbell rang. When Mrs Maréchal got up to go and answer it, one of the men pushed her back into her chair and demanded to know where her daughter was. Mrs Maréchal said nothing but her mind was a whirl of concern for Elsie, for her son Robert and for her husband Georges, who would be returning from work later.[7]

One of the men patted Mrs Maréchal down to check if she had a gun and they then led her out of the house. There was a car waiting outside and they ordered her to get in. The men then returned to the house.

A few minutes later, Elsie walked down the pavement towards her house. It all seemed so unclear, and what more could she expect to learn about the two strange men who had turned up that morning? She did not have long to find out. When she rang the doorbell, the door was opened by a man holding a pistol. Grabbing her by the arm, he dragged her into the dining room. There were now eight men sitting round the dining room table, smoking and drinking tea. One of the men snatched her handbag and emptied the contents on to the table. One of the items was a certificate showing that she was an employee of the Swedish Canteen directed by Greindl.[8]

Young Elsie came up with a story about meeting her chief at a park entrance by way of playing for time. Soon she was pushed out of the house and into a car full of GFP heavies and they took her to the entrance of the Bois de la Cambre, where she was allowed out to have her supposed meeting. When no one came, the GFP realised that they had been taken for a ride and drove her to their headquarters at rue de la Traversière.

Meanwhile, back at the Swedish Canteen, Greindl anxiously awaited Elsie's return. He was accompanied by Bidoul, Peggy van Lier and a Comet helper called Victor Michaels. Evening came and still no sign. Jean paced up and down the room, while Peggy chain-smoked. Bidoul looked on. Victor offered to go to the Maréchal house to see what was going on.

Jean paused in his pacing and weighed up the pros and cons. Victor might be able to obtain valuable information that could prevent further arrests. On the other hand, he might also fall into a trap. Eventually Jean told Victor that he could go if he promised not to attempt to enter the house.

This was Greindl's second mistake that day. Perhaps the shock of the news from Liège had upset his judgement. Perhaps as a man used to efficient management, it had still not occurred to him that his organisation was now fatally compromised. Perhaps his faith in his efficient helpers had blinded him to the reality that they were untrained and not equal to this new situation where they were directly confronted by the Gestapo. What could Victor hope to achieve if he were not to enter the house? In a situation such as this, only covert surveillance would have been able to reveal who was coming and going from the house. The house was by now under surveillance by the GFP.

Victor went down the stairs and out into the rue Ducale. It was now very dark outside. He could see the faint blue light of the tramway. He jumped on to the next tram and travelled to the penultimate stop before rue Voltaire. He walked on and took cover behind a tree from where he could see the house. It appeared to be closed up.

He kept watching for any sign of life. There was none. There would be nothing to report to Greindl, so he decided to go up to the house and ring the bell. As he approached the door, the beam of a torch broke the darkness and a voice ordered '*Hande hoch!*' Victor turned and ran into the night. A gun fired and a bullet whizzed by Victor's ear. It fired again and hit Victor. He kept running. The third shot brought him down. Victor was dead.[9]

Edith Cavell, an English nurse working in Belgium during the First World War who was an inspiration to Andrée de Jongh.

Andrée de Jongh (Dédée) in 1941. Those who met her spoke of her focus and determination. (© Marie-Pierre d'Udekem D'Acoz)

Frederick de Jongh supported the Comet line both in Brussels and later in Paris before he was arrested by the Gestapo. (© Marie-Pierre d'Udekem D'Acoz)

Jean-François Nothomb (Franco) ran the Comet line in the south of France until his arrest in January 1944. (© Marie-Pierre d'Udekem D'Acoz)

Andrée (Nadine) and Aline (Michou) Dumon. The two sisters were key players in the Comet line, as enterprising as they were brave. (© Andrée Dumon, *Je ne vous ai pas oubliés*, Éditions Mols, 2018)

Jean Greindl (Nemo) was an inspiring Comet leader who set up a sophisticated network in the Belgian regions that routed Allied airmen evaders towards Brussels.

Virginia d'Albert-Lake and her husband Philippe organised safe houses in Paris until the transfer to the Marathon safe areas.

The Avro Lancaster was one of the most successful British bombers of the Second World War but, like all bombers, it was vulnerable to both flak and night fighters. (Ronnie Macdonald / Wikimedia Commons)

A Boeing B-17 Flying Fortress. USAF heavy bombers such as these began high-altitude daylight raids over Europe from August 1942. (© Colin / Wikimedia Commons / CC BY-SA 4.0)

A Messerschmitt Bf 110 night fighter showing an array of radar antennae that guided it towards Allied bombers. (Bundesarchiv, Bild 101I-360-2095-23 / Wanderer, W. / Wikimedia Commons / CC-BY-SA 3.0)

The Westland Lysander was originally designed as an Army spotter plane but became famous for its daring use by RAF No. 161 (Special Duties) Squadron to drop and collect agents from occupied Europe. (Paul Maritz CC SA 3.0/Wikimedia Commons)

A Fairmile Motor Gun Boat similar to those that were used to collect evaders from the coast of Normandy during Operation Shelburne. (US National Archives (NAID 44267259)/Wikimedia Commons)

7

Arrest, Escape and Deportation

At the Swedish Canteen they waited in vain for Victor's return. For some reason, they concluded that if no one had reported back all must be well. Peggy van Lier went back to her house to get some sleep and woke at 4 a.m. the next morning. She had an arrangement to meet Elvire Morelle at the train station. Peggy took a tram to the rue Ducale and climbed the stairs to Greindl's office. She told him that she wanted to go round to Victor Michiel's house to find out what was going on. Jean told her that she might fall into a trap set by the Gestapo. Peggy replied that she had a good alibi. She knew that Victor's sister was a student at Louvain. She could say that she had come round to ask her about the course. She told Jean that it might be possible for her to find out about Victor and about Elsie Maréchal. It was typical of the spirit of the Comet line helpers that they did not hang back. Each of them wanted to support their colleagues even if it meant putting themselves at risk.[1]

Peggy duly made her way to the rue Ducale where the Michiels family lived. She carried out an initial surveillance of the house from the outside and, not having seen anything suspicious, she went up to the door and rang the doorbell. The door was opened by a man she did not recognise. He asked her to come in and then closed the door behind her. Then he asked Peggy if she wanted to see anyone. Peggy answered that she had come to see her friend Josie Michiels. The man then grabbed her by the arm and dragged her into the sitting room. There she found Mr and Mrs Michiels and their daughter Josie guarded by two Germans.

One of the men took Peggy's handbag from her and emptied it on the table. A man asked her what she wanted. She told him that she had come to borrow some philosophy course notes from her friend Josie. The man told her that she was lying and that she had come to meet Victor Michiels. Peggy protested that she did not know Josie's brothers. The man told her that she would be made to talk and he told her to sit down. One can only imagine the atmosphere: a mixture of fear and grief as the Michiels family contemplated the loss of their son and brother as well as their fate as his assumed accomplices.

Just after midday a car arrived to take Peggy to the rue Charles Legrelle, the Brussels headquarters of the Abwehr. Her captors told her that Victor had been shot dead. Then they led her to a room full of detainees awaiting interrogation.

One after another, Comet agents continued to fall into the Gestapo web. No one who had been caught could get away to spread the alarm and the limitations of the Comet organisation in these circumstances were laid bare. No wonder that Airey Neave at MI9 in London was losing sleep at the prospect of the line being compromised. Soon, yet another Comet helper would be added to the Gestapo's haul.

Elvire Morelle arrived at the Gare du Midi at 5 a.m. on the Paris train. She waited for three hours until the curfew was lifted before taking a tram to the rue Voltaire. It was cold and there was still ice on the ground. She had a suitcase as well as her handbag and she also carried a package that she planned to leave for her brother Charlie at the St-Gilles prison, where he was being held. As she approached, she saw a Belgian policeman. She hesitated but as the policeman showed no reaction she carried on. When she reached the door, a German GFP suddenly appeared holding a pistol. She tried to pretend that the was at the wrong address but the man told her not to move and others came up behind her.

They pushed Elvire through the door of the house and into the sitting room. It stank of stale cigarettes and the table was strewn with empty bottles and dirty cups. In due course, a truck arrived to take her to the rue Charles Legrelle. She was taken up the stairs and into an office where a man in Luftwaffe uniform sat behind a desk. He gave her a cold look. Behind him were portraits of Hitler and of Göring, holding a jewel-encrusted baton of office.

One of the men who had been in the house came in and deposited her handbag, suitcase and package on the table. The Luftwaffe officer began to open the package and took out some jam pots, which he put aside. Then he opened the suitcase, which he searched. Not finding anything of interest, he then turned to the handbag, which he emptied on to the table. Bank notes, loose change and other items fell on to the table, including a missal. The officer picked up the missal and flicked through the pages. Some prayer cards fell out from between the pages as well as a piece of folded paper. Elvire's heart missed a beat and an ice-cold chill travelled up her spine, although she fought to retain her composure. The folded note on the table contained details of the Paris flat in rue Oudinot that Frederick and Andrée de Jongh used as a safe house. The future of the Comet line hung in the balance.[2]

The officer picked up the piece of paper and began to slowly unfold it. As he did so, he looked at Elvire who maintained an expression of blank indifference. After a pause, the officer folded the note and placed it on top of the holy images before turning to open a filing cabinet. Elvire seized her opportunity, picked up the note, screwed it into a ball and put it into her mouth, swallowing it with some difficulty. The officer turned back to the desk with a dossier and the interrogation began.

After young Elsie arrived at rue de la Traversière, she was violently interrogated. Georges Maréchal was brought in and they were both taken to St-Gilles prison. The two managed to give each other a hug before being separated and taken to their separate cells. Young Elsie lay in the dark, unable to sleep due to a blinding headache, and trying to work out a plan for what would happen next. The following morning, she saw her mother when they were both taken to the prison office to complete formalities before being placed in separate cells for solitary confinement without food. For young Elsie this was the prelude to sixteen brutal interrogation sessions. In one session she was beaten repeatedly on her back for hours on end and as a result would not be able to sleep on her back for the next six months. She was also punched in the eye. In due course young Elsie was taken to the prison doctor, who ordered the interrogations to stop while her wounds were treated.[3]

During this period the prison filled with Comet associates and helpers as the GFP and Gestapo continued to make arrests. On 15 April 1943, Elsie, young Elsie and Georges Maréchal were taken before a military tribunal where, after cursory deliberations, they were sentenced to death. They were permitted to ask for grace before being returned to St-Gilles prison. Robert Maréchal had been released after several harsh interrogations when he succeeded in persuading his interrogators that he was just a young lad from school who knew nothing about what was going on.

On New Year's Day 1944, young Elsie and her mother were taken out of St-Gilles prison and began the long journey through German labour and concentration camps. Having been condemned to death, they became part of the Nacht und Nebel, or Night and Fog, programme whereby undesirable prisoners were gradually worn down by privation and enforced work. Crammed into cells at Aix-la-Chapelle, they were then forced into railway wagons. On arrival at Düsseldorf, they were stripped naked for disinfection and then continued via Frankfurt and Nuremberg until they arrived at the convict prison of Waldheim near Dresden. Here their heads were shaved and they were given convict costumes and wooden sandals. They were informed that they had no rights as condemned people and would receive no correspondence or parcels. Although the wounds on young Elsie's back were treated by the prison doctor, she was beaten again by so-called nurses. She then developed scarlet fever. In June 1944, news percolated into the prison that the Allies had landed in Normandy and there was little that the prison guards could do to control the inmates' elation. At the end of the month, they were put on a train to Leipzig, where they spent the night crowded into a small room before being forced to run for a train in the morning. The next stop was Potsdam, where a grisly prison awaited them before they were sent on to Lübeck via Hamburg. They then travelled along Germany's Baltic coast and crossed the border into Poland, where they passed through Beslau, Stettin, Danzig, Thorn and Posen and arrived at the convict prison of Ortburg. Again, they were forced into a cramped cell with little ventilation and a single pail for sanitation.

In the late summer, there was news that Paris had been liberated by the Allies. The prisoners danced with joy and were punished for three days without either food or exercise. As Allied victory became ever more certain, the SS became even more ruthless. The next stop for young Elsie, her mother and their companions was Ravensbrück concentration camp. Constructed by order of Heinrich Himmler in November 1938, Ravensbrück was designed exclusively for women. The new arrivals were greeted with a message on the gates of the camp: *Arbeit macht free*, or 'work sets you free'. The reality was that of 130,000 women who arrived at the camp during the war, 50,000 died either from the conditions or by execution. By March 1944, the Russian advance was close enough for the camp organisers to take action. The inmates were duly marched out to a station, where they were put in cattle trucks for transport to Mauthausen concentration camp.[4]

However, while the camp organisers worked relentlessly to ensure the extermination of their inmates, others were working equally hard to find ways of saving them. The Red Cross had engaged in extended negotiations to remove survivors so that the camp commandant would be unable to carry out his plan of gassing them before the Allied forces could relieve them. It was touch and go but in due course a fleet of white Red Cross lorries appeared and the inmates were marched out of the camp. Each person was guided to their seat by a kindly Red Cross worker and provided with a blanket. The agony of young Elsie and her mother at last seemed to be over. As the lorries drove off, the sun was shining, and nature seemed to join the celebration with all the colours of spring on display. Once the convoy had crossed the border into Switzerland, despite last-ditch attempts by Nazi border guards to detain them, the Maréchal mother and daughter made their way as fast as possible to Brussels to be reunited with Robert and other relations.

8

Dark Clouds

In November 1942, Peggy van Lier sat in her cell wondering what would happen next. An interrogation was more than likely. Would it also be violent? How much did they already know? Where was Elsie Maréchal? Had they yet discovered Comet HQ at the Swedish Canteen? Would she, like so many others, be deported to a concentration camp and spend months if not years trying to retain a grip on life with her fingernails? There was a sound outside and a German soldier unlocked her cell door. He beckoned to Peggy and when she went over to him, heart in her mouth, he told her that she was free to go. Peggy looked at him in blank astonishment and then grasped his hand. 'Thank you!' she said. When she left the building, she walked to the nearest church and, kneeling in a pew, she said a prayer of thanksgiving. Then she went back to her house, opened a bottle of wine and drank three glasses.[1]

Peggy went round to the Swedish Canteen to brief Jean Greindl. His advice was clear – she needed to get away from Brussels and preferably find a way to England. It was more than likely that, as the Gestapo put two and two together, they would be back for her and next time it was unlikely that she would be so lucky. There were others that Greindl considered to be in danger and so, when Peggy boarded the train at the Gare du Midi bound for Paris, she was accompanied by Georges d'Oultremont and his cousin Edouard. Georges was a Belgian Army officer who had become involved in Comet line operations but was now on the Gestapo most-wanted list. He was an example of just how tenuous the situation had become for Comet. He accompanied Dédée to the south and then over the Pyrenees to Spain and then to Gibraltar. When he reached England, he took up parachute training and would later return to the fray when he parachuted back into France in October 1943. There was now no more havering on the part of Greindl because the scale of the disaster was becoming clear. In about forty-eight hours, more than 100 Comet line helpers or their associates and relations had been arrested by the Gestapo. The number of arrests exceeded by a quarter the number of evaders who had escaped across the border to Spain. The Comet line and all those wittingly or unwittingly associated with it were paying a very heavy price for the freedom of Allied servicemen.

Meanwhile, Peggy was being staged through the southern Comet network, including St-Jean-de-Luz, Francia's house and the long walk over the Pyrenees accompanied by Florentino and Dédée, protected by the inky darkness. They eventually reached Irun, where they were picked up by a local garage owner. The next day a British Embassy car appeared and Peggy and her companions were taken to Madrid. They stayed there for three weeks while arrangements were made for their onward passage to England. Then they drove to Jerez de la Frontera, where they were each given a bottle of sherry and advised to drink it all before they got to the Spanish frontier, lest it be confiscated by customs. After arriving in the safe haven of Gibraltar, Peggy waited for a flight that took her to England, where she was met by MI9 representative Jimmy Langley. With her flaming red hair, Peggy obviously made an impression for the two fell in love and would later get married. Georges and Edouard took a somewhat less romantic trip to Liverpool by sea via the Azores. They were also met by Langley at Liverpool docks. He took them to dinner at a French restaurant before driving them to 'patriotic school' in Wandsworth, London. This establishment was designed to weed out any foreign agents posing as evaders.

Peggy's release by the Gestapo seems somewhat extraordinary in the circumstances. The Gestapo were running amok among the Comet line helpers and there seemed little reason why they would not have grilled her along with the rest. It may have been that Peggy had done enough to convince her captors that she had indeed come round to the Michiels' house by chance and that her alibi of borrowing college notes was convincing.

Having got their foot in the door, the Gestapo made the most of their opportunities. There were so many arrests that it was impossible to be sure who might have been compromised. As could be seen with the Maréchal affair, they just had to sit and wait while Comet helpers walked into the trap. The arrests were not limited to Brussels. The Gestapo followed the Comet evasion route all the way to Paris and beyond. Frederick de Jongh was advised by his friend Robert Ayle to move his headquarters from 10 rue Oudinot. This was sound advice since the address had been sitting on the desk of a Luftwaffe interrogator before Elvire Morelle disposed of it. Frederick moved to a third-floor apartment on the rue Vaneau.

One can only begin to imagine how Frederick de Jongh must have felt. He knew that his eldest daughter, Suzanne, was a prisoner of the Nazis and that his wife was also in danger. He knew that he could not return to Brussels without facing almost certain arrest. Frederick was not the only one assailed by doubts in the face of the latest onslaught by the Gestapo against the Comet line. Jean Greindl had travelled to Paris for a meeting with the southern heads to discuss the latest developments. Dédée had also arrived in Paris, having travelled all night from the south. Everything seemed to hang in the balance. The flame of freedom was flickering and in danger of being snuffed out altogether.

Although the writing appeared to be on the wall and it only seemed a matter of time before each of them – Dédée, Frederick and Jean – received the proverbial knock on the door from the Gestapo, Dédée drew upon a message that she had received from Michael Creswell in which he assured her of the value of the work of the Comet line and how it encouraged not only the evaders themselves but also their fellow airmen back at their bases in England. They were living witnesses of the effectiveness of the escape lines and, without giving away an incriminating detail, they recounted their exciting stories of how they were rescued after being shot down, provided with shelter, food and clothing, and then accompanied on the routes that took them from Belgium to Paris and then onwards to Bayonne and the Spanish frontier. Their comrades were left in no doubt that, if they were to suffer the same fate over enemy territory, there would be committed men and women willing to risk their lives in order to help them.

This letter was a timely morale boost for the Comet line leaders as they faced the withering storm of Nazi oppression and when they had every reason to feel demoralised. It proved that their efforts were worthwhile and hugely appreciated by those whom they had sacrificed so much to help. In the gathering darkness, the flame of freedom was rekindled and they all agreed that, come what may, they would carry on with their work.

★ ★ ★

It was right that Dédée, the original inspiration of the Comet line, should be the one to reset and reinvigorate the organisation after the hammer blow that it had received in November 1941. However, this decision was made with the full knowledge of the potential costs. Another aspect of this was that Dédée also knew that one of the soldiers she was sending back to the front line was her own father. This could not have been easy for her and in due course she made it her business to try to persuade him to make the journey over the mountains and to seek safety in England. Knowing that he would not wish to be a passive observer abroad while his family was in danger in occupied Belgium and France, she argued that he could be of even greater help to the escape movement by helping to co-ordinate its work from London.

On 13 January 1943, Dédée, her father Frederick, Nothomb and three Allied evaders, one British and two American, boarded the 2130 train at Austerlitz station bound for Hendaye. When the train reached Bayonne, they were met by Elvire de Greef accompanied by three other helpers. It was pouring with rain and Elvire de Greef told them that it had been like this for ten days. This was a heavy blow for Dédée as she was keen to take the opportunity of escorting her father over the mountains to safety as soon as possible. She knew that the river would be in spate and that it would be too dangerous for a man of his age to take on such a journey. When Elvire told her that it was too risky for any of them to cross, Dédée revealed the determination that had kept her going all these months. The young servicemen would be able to manage and she was certainly not going to be put off by bad weather. When Elvire persisted, Dédée replied that she would consult with Florentino before making a final decision. She also resisted Elvire's suggestion that she might stay with her father at Elvire's house while the evaders went across the mountain with Florentino. So she bade farewell to her father and went on with the others.[2]

Dédée and the men got on some bicycles to make the journey to St-Jean-de-Luz, from where they met Florentino before making their way up the hill to Francia's house. Florentino confirmed that the weather was too severe for a crossing that night but that it would be better the following day. Florentino knew the mountains better than anyone and, although he was not one to be easily daunted, he also had enough respect for the mountains to know not to test them too far. In the sheeting rain, already perilous paths would become rivers, rocks would become slippery, and falls would not only be likely but almost certain.

Francia was nervous. She told Dédée that people had been talking. They knew that men stayed at her house before making the journey over the mountains to Spain. How long would it be before the authorities got to hear of it? She was right to worry. There were informers who could make a pretty penny from giving the authorities such valuable information. She asked that the men should stay at the back of the house but then her natural sense of hospitality took over and she invited them back to the front room where they could be by the fire and dry out after their long, wet journey. She gave them hot soup and milk.

As the group settled down, relieved not to be in motion and to be out of the cold and wet, the dog barked suddenly. There was silence and then Francia asked her son to go out of the door to see if anyone was about. In a few minutes the boy came back and spoke to his mother in Basque. Francia looked relieved and told Dédée that it was someone she knew – a farm hand who had occasionally helped with the evasion journeys. As the young man put his head round the door, Dédée's heart fell. She did indeed recognise him. When he was helping on journeys items had gone missing from her backpack. She did not trust him. The young man clocked all the men in the room and smiled. In due course he left, leaving Dédée with a sense of foreboding.

Florentino announced that he was going back to St-Jean-de-Luz to do some errands but that he would be back to escort the men the following evening. Dédée opted to stay with the men. While the airmen joked and laughed, she remained sombre. The appearance of the rogue Basque the previous evening was little compared to the concern that she felt for her father. She had a conscience that he was in danger because of her and wanted to see him safely off to England as soon as possible. Little did she know that their recent parting in the pouring rain was the last time she would see him.

Eventually the airmen went off to get some sleep and woke the next morning still in good spirits with the hope that today they would see freedom. Amid the chatter, there was the low sound of an engine in the distance and the conversation was silenced. There was not undue concern as cars could be heard occasionally in the area and one of the men made a joke about it being the Gestapo. Unfortunately for him and everyone else, it was not a joke. Dédée saw a shadow pass by a window and then the door was kicked open. First the muzzle of a machine gun and then a gendarme appeared. They shouted at everyone to put their hands up. The airmen were ordered to face a wall while the gendarmes kicked over furniture and ripped up floorboards. Their commander demanded to know where the fifth one was.

This was proof to Dédée if any were needed that they had indeed been betrayed by the farm hand for how else would they know that there had been five of them? Florentino had, of course, departed after the visit. Then they were ordered out into the cold courtyard with more shouts and threats while Francia's three children wept amid the noise and shock. They were ordered into single file with the airmen in front with their hands on their heads and Dédée and Francia behind. Then they were marched off down the wet lane towards St-Jean-de-Luz. As they came down towards the town and began to cross the bridge over the estuary, Dédée thought about jumping off the bridge to make her escape. When she looked down, however, she could see that the tide was out, revealing the rocks. They went on into the town, where they were marched to the local prison.[3]

The sad spectacle had been witnessed by many and news travelled fast. When Florentino heard that Dédée had been captured, he set off over the mountains to warn the British. The news also reached Elvire de Greef, who shared it with a broken-hearted Frederick de Jongh. Desperate with grief, he said he would go down in person to the prison and had to be dissuaded. One can only imagine the grief and remorse he felt as he thought about his daughter in a cell at the mercy of ruthless men. Despite Elvire's efforts to console him, she too knew that the prospects were grim. How long would it take for the Gestapo to discover that they had captured the prize that they had been seeking, without being clear who it was. Time was of the essence, and Elvire was not one to hang around. She began to concoct rescue plans that with hindsight seem desperate and in other circumstances might have seemed almost comical, but they revealed the love and loyalty that Dédée inspired in her followers and friends as well as the sheer determination of those responsible for keeping the flame of the Comet line alive.

Dédée had been moved to the prison in Bayonne called the Villa Chagrin and, when Nothomb had returned from Paris to join Elvire, they sat in cafes outside the prison walls and dreamed up their schemes. One involved talking to a woman who worked in the prison and another a rope with a grapple to be thrown over the prison wall. The rope proved not to be long enough and in any case the plan was vague about how to break into Dédée's cell and get her back over the wall unseen.

Dédée, meanwhile, was taken from the prison to be interrogated by the Gestapo and then returned afterwards. One thing became clear. The Germans still had little idea who she was or what her significance was in the organisation of the Comet escape line. Little did they guess that she was its leader and inspiration.

9

Retribution

It seemed as if the Comet line and the whole spirit of resistance in both Belgium and France were on the receiving end of a relentless assault by an apparently omnipotent foe. Moreover, it seemed that it was only a matter of time before the entire escape line system would be vanquished, with any flickering flames of resistance guttering and dying in the squalor of the concentration camps. The arrests had far-reaching effects that extended to London. Those such as Airey Neave and Jimmy Langley who worked at MI9 found themselves on the back foot as they tried to defend their work with the escape lines, which many regarded as peripheral to the war effort. While the aircrew themselves deeply appreciated the sacrifice and efforts that had enabled them to return to active duty in Britain, the wider intelligence community regarded the escape lines as unreliable and prone to infiltration by enemy agents. What was maddening for those who supported the escape lines was that in many ways their critics in London were right. As had been shown, amateur escape organisations could so easily be penetrated by informers and traitors posing either as helpers or as evaders.[1]

While MI9 under Brigadier Norman Crockatt fought for its raison d'être among the London-based intelligence community, and while other organisations such as the SOE also suffered infiltration by the Gestapo, on the ground in occupied Belgium and France the flame of freedom did not die. It was rekindled by those committed to fighting without arms, notably Jean-François Nothomb, 'Franco', who would largely take over Comet line southern operations after the arrest of Dédée. January 1943, however, ended with a somewhat different style of resistance as when the Gestapo headquarters in Brussels were attacked in a daring and unauthorised raid.

Baron Jean de Selys Longchamps had served in the Belgian Army as a cavalry officer with the 1er Regiment des Guides, an armoured reconnaissance regiment. Having escaped to England via Dunkirk in 1940, he returned to France in the hope of joining the fight in a reformed French Army. However, after the surrender of French forces, he found himself escaping south with many others and he was interned in Marseilles. Having escaped imprisonment, he made his way to Spain and eventually back to England, where he joined the RAF. He was posted to 609 Squadron, which included some of his fellow countrymen and was equipped with the Hawker Typhoon.[2] Powered by a Napier Sabre engine, the most powerful piston engine developed during the Second World War, the single-engine fighter-bomber was armed with twelve .0303 Browning machine guns. Some versions were fitted with cannon and they could also carry rockets for ground attack missions.

Jean's father, Baron Raymond de Selys Longchamps, had served with distinction in the First World War, where he won Belgian and French bravery awards and the British Military Cross.[3] Jean was equally determined to make his mark by resisting the Nazi occupation of his country. The Gestapo headquarters in Brussels was located in a tall art deco building with bow windows at 453 avenue Louise, which at the time stood out from the lower residential buildings on either side. Located on the southern side of Brussels, avenue Louise was approached by wide avenues, making it easily visible and accessible from the air.

Jean asked the permission of his superiors to carry out a raid on the building but was not given clearance, although it remained under consideration. The RAF had carried out an attack on Gestapo headquarters in Oslo in 1942 and would execute similar missions later in the war. On 31 October 1944 twenty-five Mosquito light bombers would attack Gestapo headquarters located in the buildings of the University of Aarhus in Denmark. On 21 March 1945, Mosquitoes would attack Gestapo headquarters in Copenhagen located in the Shell offices known as the Shellhus. However, for Jean de Selys Longchamps this matter was personal, and he was not inclined to wait for formal permission from his superiors. He set about planning his attack and saw his opportunity when he was sent on an operational sortie against railway junctions near Brussels. Taking off from Manston airfield in Kent on 20 January with his wingman, Flight Sergeant Blanco, Jean set a course over the Channel before attacking the designated targets. He had taken care to ensure that his aircraft carried the maximum amount of ammunition so that he had plenty left after his official targets were destroyed. He was also carrying a bundle of Belgian flags. Once his operational objectives had been achieved, Jean told his wingman to head back to base. Meanwhile, he set a course for Brussels, only a few miles away. Flying at low altitude to avoid German radar and fighter interception, he approached the south of Brussels and took his bearings on landmarks that were familiar to him. Balancing the aircraft and flattening out, he flew up the wide avenue towards his target. Soon the art deco bow front was in his sights. He held his fire to minimise the risk of collateral damage to residential buildings and then he pressed the firing button. Twelve machine guns blazed and raked the building from top to bottom, bullets smashing into glass and pulverising concrete before the Typhoon roared overhead. Jean opened his canopy and threw out a Belgian flag before flying over the royal palace and the home of an aristocratic relation, where he threw out more flags before setting a course for base.

After landing back at Manston, Jean de Selys Longchamps received a dressing down from senior officers for disobeying orders. However, not long afterwards he was awarded the Distinguished Flying Cross, which included the Gestapo raid in the citation. The attack had killed the head of the SD in Brussels along with other senior Gestapo officers and two others, as well as causing several casualties. The building was put out of action for about six weeks. The greatest damage was perhaps to German prestige. De Selys Longchamps did not know that young Elise Maréchal had been beaten by the Gestapo and her family sent off to concentration camps, but this glimpse of a knight in shining armour may have given a spark of hope to those who were on the receiving end of unrelenting terror and subjugation. It may also have been fitting that an evader who had escaped through Spain to England should come back and leave his calling card. Jean died in August 1943 after his aircraft crashed when landing at Manston and his fellow countrymen erected a memorial outside the building in avenue Louise to acknowledge his act of resistance.

Meanwhile, the Gestapo continued to track down Comet line organisers and helpers and, as January gave way to February, the next person in their sights was Jean Greindl. After the meeting in Paris with Dédée and Frederick de Jongh, Greindl had returned to Brussels. Dédée had explained to him that it was only a matter of time before he, too, was arrested and Jean had merely smiled, as if resigned to his fate. She had implored him not to return to the Swedish Canteen and vowed to arrange a replacement for him so that he could escape to safety in England. However, Dédée herself was in danger and found it difficult to persuade Greindl to do something that she would not be prepared to do herself. Greindl had no illusions. His wife had just given birth to a son, their second child, and, more concerned about his family's safety than his own, he arranged to visit them in secret. His wife implored him to go to England but he was determined to carry on.

In London, following the capture of Dédée, Airey Neave and his associates at MI9 were desperate to make contact with Greindl. There was a resounding silence emanating from Brussels as the Gestapo rampage continued. Neave was determined to send in two communications specialists to help Greindl regain contact with London and to help rebuild the shattered escape line. The Belgian Air Attaché in London suggested a soldier in the Belgian Army in Britain, Sergeant Henri Decat. He was given a cover name of Lieutenant Drew and sent off for specialist training, including parachute insertion into enemy territory as well as signalling and codes. Decat would be accompanied by another Belgian, known as Lieutenant Boeuf. The men were given money and false identity cards as well as instructions to put themselves at the disposal of Greindl. They flew from RAF Tempsford near Bedford in a Halifax bomber of 161 Squadron RAF.[4]

Along with 138 Squadron, 161 Squadron was part of the RAF Special Duties Service. Its main role was to carry out missions on behalf of the SOE and the Secret Intelligence Service (SIS), including agent drops and collections as well as supply drops. They flew specially adapted aircraft and operated from designated airfields that were shrouded in secrecy. Not only did the Special Duties Service drop agents by parachute, it also landed on specially designated fields in occupied Europe to both drop and collect agents. Such missions required a special breed of pilot who could fly solo and without wireless aids for navigation. The Westland Lysander was the aircraft used for such flights and it could take a maximum of three passengers and their luggage, although four passengers are known to have been carried. Originally designed as an army spotter and liaison aircraft, the Lysander had proved to be too slow and vulnerable in contested airspace but its low speed and ability to take off and land in confined spaces made it ideal for covert operations. It was also built ruggedly, which helped it to withstand the rough landings to which it was often subjected. To minimise the dangers from enemy flak or night fighters, the Lysanders were painted matt black and were often flown at low altitude to get under enemy radar cover.

Lysander pilots were trained to identify visual points on the ground such as bends in rivers or reliably lit installations such as prison camps. They carried specially prepared maps that they could unfold with one hand for each leg of the journey. These maps showed the routes that had been planned to avoid enemy flak installations. On arrival at the location, which would have been prepared by a ground team, there would be an exchange of a code letter in Morse for security verification and the pilot would then fly over the field before making his approach for landing. The landing zone would be marked out by a simple arrangement of flashlights arranged in an inverted 'L'. Turnaround was extremely rapid. Having reached the flashlight at the end of the field, the pilot would bring the aircraft around and taxi back to the two flashlights at the beginning of the field. His passenger or passengers would then climb down, handing down any packages, and any new passengers would climb in. This would all take place in under three minutes. The aircraft would then take off again.[5]

Other aircraft used by the Special Duties Service included the Lockheed Hudson, Handley Page Halifax and Short Stirling. The twin-engine Hudson had a crew of three, including a navigator and wireless operator, which enabled the pilot to concentrate on the flying. Although the Hudson was a much larger aircraft than the Lysander and needed a longer landing ground, the Special Duties Squadron pilots managed to minimise the space required to take off and land. The Hudson was used for pick-ups in enemy territory and it could also carry 'C-type' supply containers. The Halifax and later the Stirling were only used for aerial drops of agents or supplies and both could carry much greater numbers of C-type containers.

Pilots of the Special Duties squadrons were chosen for their initiative and ability to think for themselves alongside their proven flying skills. Squadron leader Guy Lockhart was a case in point. Lockhart had flown Spitfires before being posted to 138 Squadron in November 1941. In February 1942 he was then transferred to 161 Special Duties Squadron based at Tangmere to fly the Lysander. Although some of Lockhart's missions passed without undue incident, there were many close calls. When he landed to deliver the agent Gilbert Renault-Meulier (Rémy) on 26 March 1942, his aircraft ran into ploughed ground at the end of the landing strip and was only freed with considerable difficulty. A month later he came in to land near Chateauroux to discover too late that the landing lights had been set on an ascending slope.[6] The impact caused the engine to burst into flames but fortunately the fire extinguished itself before any further damage could be caused. Lockhart was able to take off again with two passengers. After this incident it was decided that landing team leaders should in future be trained in England before being allowed to designate landing fields. However, on 23 August 1942, when delivering the Belgian agent William Ugeaux, the landing field was set on a descending slope. This time Lockhart had to switch off the engine to prevent the Lysander from running off the end. On 31 August Lockhart landed at Aubigny with one passenger. As the aircraft was taxiing, it ran into a grass-covered ditch, which broke the undercarriage. Lockhart waited for his passenger to get out of the area before setting the aircraft alight with an incendiary bomb. He then made his own escape. He was passed down an escape line that arranged for him to be picked up by a Polish felucca off Narbonne and he was then taken to Gibraltar and returned to England on 13 September. He was airborne again on 18 November 1942 with two passengers and various packages. Heavy cloud meant that he had to abort the mission but as he emerged from the cloud he ran into seven Focke-Wulf Fw 190s. The Fw 190 was a formidable aircraft, one of the best fighter planes of the war. An unarmed Lysander would not stand a chance against one Fw 190, let alone seven. Lockhart managed to dive into cloud with the fighters in pursuit. He then descended to sea level and somehow managed to make his escape. On another mission Lockhart had a problem that forced him to fly home using some creative flying techniques, controlling the pitch of the plane by use of the throttle. Lockhart was then transferred to the newly formed 627 Squadron based at RAF Oakington in Cambridgeshire to fly de Havilland Mosquito twin-engine light bombers. He then transferred to 692 Squadron as its commander. The squadron continued to develop the use of the Mosquito, including accurate dropping of 4,000lb bombs and minelaying. He then moved to 7 Squadron to fly Avro Lancaster bombers with the Pathfinders. He was killed during a raid on Friedrichshafen on 27–28 April 1944.

The attempt by MI9 to shore up Jean Greindl's operation in Brussels proved to be short-lived. The only message that MI9 received after Decat had been successfully inserted was that Greindl had been arrested by the Gestapo on 6 February. Apparently, he had been in his office when four armed men burst through the door. He was taken to the rue Charles Legrelle, where he was shocked to see his wife, who had also been arrested. MI9 received more details on the arrest from Jean's brother Albert, who had managed to escape across the Pyrenees with a party of evading American airmen, guided by Florentino. Greindl was taken to an army barracks at Etterbeek and on 29 April 1943 he was condemned to death. While he was awaiting execution, on 7 September the barracks was bombed by Allied aircraft in a routine air raid and Greindl was killed instantly.[7]

The Bright New Recruit

As we have seen with Harry Cole and the Pat O'Leary line, the escape lines were plagued by traitors and informers who could wreak havoc, leading to the imprisonment or execution of organisers and helpers as well as long spells in PoW camps for the evaders. For some of those Nazi collaborators, their work was a logical development from a life of crime and deceit. They were indifferent to such ideals as national loyalty and instead worked for the highest bidder. Such were Harold Cole and Prosper Dezitter. For others, collaboration was a matter of genuine loyalty to new masters who gave them a purpose in life. Such was Jacques Desoubrie, alias Jean Masson, alias Pierre Boulain.

Desoubrie was the illegitimate son of a Belgian doctor who was later abandoned by his mother. With no real roots or loyalty, feeling shunned by the society into which he was born, he welcomed the arrival of the Nazis who drove that society into subjection. The tables were turned and he was keen to be on the winning side and to ensure that his new masters maintained the upper hand. Desoubrie was short and stocky with fair hair and piercing grey eyes. He began his work for the Gestapo by infiltrating resistance organisations in northern France and it was during this period that he came to the attention of Robert Ayle, a close confidant of Frederick de Jongh. It was not long before Ayle introduced the man he knew as Jean Masson to Frederick.

Following the arrest of Dédée, and with two of his daughters now imprisoned by the Nazis, Frederick was determined to continue with the Comet line operations to honour Dédée while also frantically trying to find intermediaries who could intercede for her to the Germans. He approached the Swiss authorities and the British but the latter, seeing the complications that this could cause for the surviving members of the Comet line, including Frederick himself, were reluctant to get involved. The loss of Dédée had also caused an interruption in the flow of evaders from Paris to the south. This meant that safe houses were overcrowded, increasing the risk of discovery. This problem would be resolved once Jean-François Nothomb took full control of the southern operations. Things had also become more difficult in the north with more stringent customs checks and less chance of evaders getting through on the pretext that they were Flemish or deaf mutes. In his enthusiasm to get the Comet line running again, Frederick was open to any help that he could get.

Robert Ayle's contact seemed to be full of ideas as to how to improve the situation. He told Frederick that he had a friend who had managed to obtain blank passes as used by workmen who needed to cross the border. Even better, he had a copy of the Feldgendarmerie stamp for the Lille customs area. He was confident that producing a list of false names for the evaders as they passed through would not be a problem. This all sounded plausible and Frederick was keen to give the new man a try. He offered him a trial run.

An arrangement was made in May for Masson to escort evaders from Brussels to Paris. In due course, Masson appeared at the Gare du Nord accompanied by seven evaders. The men were then allocated safe houses organised by Comet helper Madeleine Bouteloupt, pending their onward journey to the south. The new recruit had passed his first test with flying colours.

As May tuned to June, Masson was once again in touch. He announced that he had another group of evaders and was anxious that they should be met at the Gare du Nord on 7 June. As it was such a large party, he stressed that all the Comet helpers should be there to meet them. His manner had changed and it sounded to

Frederick that Masson was now calling the shots. However, in his eagerness to get the line moving again, he chose to overlook it.

Frederick set about making arrangements to meet and escort the new arrivals. He sent Madeleine Bouteloupt and another Comet helper called Raymonde on the train to Lille, where they would meet Masson and his group. Masson was already waiting when they arrived and he allocated one evader to each of the two women. While they awaited the arrival of the Paris train, Raymonde chose to leave the station and sit in a bar nearby with her evader. No sooner had they sat down and ordered coffees than she felt a hand on her shoulder and looked up to see that they were surrounded by Gestapo agents. Meanwhile, the Paris train arrived and Madeleine and her companion got on the train. She was unaware of what had happened to Raymonde. In due course some men appeared in her carriage and asked to see her identity card. One of the men retained it and she and her companion were arrested. Madeleine was taken to a separate carriage, where she was searched by a female Gestapo agent who slapped her across the face.

The train continued to Paris, where by now Frederick, Robert Ayle and his wife Germaine were getting ready to meet the new party of evaders. They waited by the platform as the train pulled in and then saw Masson step down, smiling genially, accompanied by a group of rather self-conscious men. As they gathered, gendarmes suddenly appeared from nowhere and they were surrounded. Handcuffs were produced and the whole group was led off towards the railway police station. Frederick, Robert, Germaine and Masson sat on a bench along with the evaders until they were all led away to waiting cars outside the station. Frederick, Robert and Germaine travelled separately from Masson and the other men and they were driven to the rue des Saussaies. They were then taken to a waiting room, where they sat, pondering their fate. Then the door opened and Masson appeared. He was no longer handcuffed and he sneered at them, his manner full of contempt for those who dared to resist the new masters to whom he had given his loyalty.[1]

Eight days after the arrest of Frederick de Jongh in June 1943, Jean-François Nothomb visited his flat to check if there were any incriminating documents. The flat had been sealed by the Gestapo but Jean-François managed to get in and he gathered together as many false identity cards and other documents as he could. It was a calculated risk and might have got him arrested.

Jean-François was undeterred by the arrest of Frederick and other Comet leaders and helpers. On the contrary, he was spurred on to even greater efforts to ensure that the line ran smoothly and effectively and he certainly had no lack of customers. As the Allied bombing campaign continued and intensified, a continuous flow of airmen was passed down the line, eager to make their way to freedom. Jean-François ran regular fortnightly trips between Paris and Bilbao but, in addition to the threat posed by informers, security had also increased at main stations such as the Gare Austerlitz, the Paris gateway to the south. As the pressure increased, Jean-François decided to use an alternative route, first taking a train to Bordeaux and then using a local line to Dax, north-east of Bayonne. Bicycles were placed near the station so that the evaders could ride with Jean-François to the safe house at Anglet. After the long train journey, the evaders were usually treated to a meal at a restaurant in Dax. This had been one of Dédée's methods for calming the nerves of the evaders. Well-fed and content, they were hopefully less likely to compromise themselves or their helpers. However, the evaders only had to make the journey once; Jean-François had to repeat it over and again and also had to carry the responsibility for all the arrangements, tickets, false identity papers and so on. As if the train journeys were not enough, there was also the arduous physical climb up steep mountain paths in all weathers and mostly at night. The potential for accidents or discovery by German or Spanish guards was a constant threat.

Aware of his tireless efforts, the British arranged for Jean-François to have a break, partly as an opportunity to recover his strength but also to thank him officially for his work and for that of all the Comet line organisers and helpers. Airey Neave hoped to persuade him to come back to England, anxious as he was to avoid another incident such as had befallen Andrée de Jongh. After a meeting with Jean-François on 28 September, Michael Creswell drove him to Madrid in his diplomatic Bentley and then on to Gibraltar via Malaga. Before they reached the border at La Linea, Jean-François was put in the boot so as to avoid any unwelcome questions at the checkpoint. Spain was crawling with pro-Nazi agents and the Spanish authorities were inclined to be suspicious, so it was important to keep things as quiet as possible, especially since Jean-François would need to come back again.

When he stepped out of the boot of the Bentley, Jean-François found himself in a different world. He was no longer in occupied Europe and the soldiers who snapped to attention were not about to arrest him. The Military Intelligence officers he met were not about to interrogate him. As he looked out over the bay and strait of Gibraltar, he knew that the seas were controlled by friendly ships and even the air felt free.[2]

Gibraltar's role had evolved during the war. From 1940, it had been the base for the formidable Force H, under the command of Admiral James Somerville. Force H had the unpleasant task of confronting the French fleet at Mers-el-Kébir to prevent it falling into German hands. It would sour Anglo-French relations for years to come.[3] Force H had answered Churchill's dramatic call to sink the *Bismarck* by sending HMS *Ark Royal* with her Fairey Swordfish torpedo planes along with the battleship HMS *Renown* and the cruiser HMS *Sheffield*. Although antiquated in appearance, one of the Swordfish torpedoes had damaged *Bismarck*'s rudder enough to make it a sitting duck for approaching Royal Navy battleships. Force H had then become heavily involved in the Battle of the Mediterranean, fighting mainly against the Italian fleet. It had escorted convoys to Malta and run the gauntlet of the Italian Regia Aeronautica and the German X Fliegerkorps. By now Operation Torch, the invasion of North Africa, was over and General Dwight D. Eisenhower, who had commanded operations from Gibraltar, was no longer present. He had been busy planning the invasion of Sicily in July 1943 and the invasion of mainland Italy in September, having also announced the surrender of the Italian fleet. The Rock continued to play an important role in all these operations, providing escorts and supplies while it held open the gateway to the Mediterranean for Allied forces.

Apart from Michael Creswell (Monday) who had driven him from Madrid, Airey Neave and Colonel Cecil Rait, both of MI9, had flown from England via Lisbon. Donald Darling, perhaps the most experienced British intelligence expert in the Iberian Peninsula, was their host. The Governor, Lieutenant General Sir Noel Mason-MacFarlane, formally thanked Jean-François and the Comet line on behalf of His Majesty the King and Jean-François told them how his visit to the Rock had given him renewed hope.[4]

Neave discussed his new plans for creating safe havens for airmen in the forests of Belgium and France and also a daring escape plan by sea from Britanny called Operation Shelburne. This operation would prove to be one of the surprise success stories in the history of Second World War escape operations. As both the Pat O'Leary line and the Comet line were compromised or limited in their operations by the corrosive effects of informers and by the increased Allied bombing of railways in the approach to D-Day, Operation Shelburne was conceived as a way of rescuing men from the north of France and taking them by sea directly back to England. The Comet line had been created on the basis that rescue for evaders from the northern coasts was not a viable option due to the level of restrictions imposed by the Germans in the coastal areas. Shelburne somehow managed to be the exception that proved the rule.

The Shelburne operation was created from the ashes of a previous operation named Oaktree. This operation went wrong from the start. Two agents, Vladamir Bourysoukine and Raymond Labrosse, were parachuted into France in March 1943 to set up the operation but their radio was damaged in the jump, making it impossible to communicate with London. Bourysoukine first made an unsuccessful attempt to carry out a rescue operation in Britanny and then took a party of evaders south. Against advice from MI9, he contacted previous members of the Pat line and soon the Oaktree line was penetrated by the Gestapo agent Roger le Neveu. Labrosse managed to return to England, where he immediately set about convincing MI9 that the escape plan from Brittany was still feasible. MI9 agreed and appointed another French Canadian, Lucien Dumais, to lead a reformed line to be called Shelburne. Dumais was a sergeant major in the Canadian Fusiliers Mont Royal and a commando. He had been captured at Dieppe but managed to escape and made his way to Marseilles. After a tour in North Africa, he was recruited for special duties. On 10–11 November 1943, Dumais and Labrosse were flown to France in two Lysanders of 161 (Special Duties) Squadron, piloted by Squadron Leader Hugh Verity and Pilot Officer Marc McCairns, to a field near Soissons. The Lysanders returned to England with five aircrew evaders and an agent.[5]

Dumais and Labrosse set up safe houses in Paris to act as the main collection point for evaders. They then travelled to Britanny, where they made contact with resistance leaders on the coast and set up safe houses in local villages. They chose the beach at Ause Cochab, code name Bonaparte, for the pick-ups. Rather than transport the evaders in small groups, they were taken in a truck, posing as foreign workers on the Atlantic Wall. They were given suitable false IDs and special passes for the restricted coastal area. Getting the evaders into the area was an achievement in itself but the maritime side of the operation was also highly challenging. The Brittany coast was surrounded by hidden rocks and there were powerful currents. The weather was unpredictable and the rise and fall of the tide had to be carefully anticipated to get small boats into shore.

The Royal Navy unit tasked with picking up the evaders from the Britanny beaches was 15th Motor Gun Boat Flotilla. Operating mainly from Dartmouth, the flotilla was part of Royal Navy coastal forces that also operated Motor Torpedo Boats (MTBs) and Motor Launches (MLs). These were used in operations such as attacking enemy shipping or intercepting blockade runners. The arrival of a Motor Gun Boat (MGB) near the coast was signalled the day before by a coded message broadcast on the BBC. The evaders were then led to the coast, where they lay low until the surf boats from the MGB approached the beach. They would then file down to the beach, avoiding any mines that had been previously identified and marked. The surf boats then took the evaders back to the MGB, which returned to England. Great care was taken to muffle oars in the surf boats and the MGB itself had an anchor rope made of woven grass to make it more silent and easier to cut in an emergency. These daring operations were carried out eight times right under the noses of German coastal batteries nearby. A total of 136 evaders were taken off the beach, 94 of whom were from USAAF and the others were from the RCAF, RAF as well as SAS teams, agents and other civilians. The 15th MGB Flotilla also carried out operations involving SOE agents from other beaches.[6]

Needless to say, Nothomb would not be persuaded to fly to England and in due course he climbed back into the boot of the Bentley for the return over the border.

Meltdown

Arrangements were made to replace Jean Greindl with a new head called Count Antoine d'Ursel, who worked under the cover name of Jacques Cartier. Although d'Ursel set about assiduously creating a team of helpers, he had an uphill struggle against the depredations of Jean Masson who, having disposed of Frederick de Jongh, had moved to Brussels to continue his nefarious work.

D'Ursel was forced to work outside Brussels, taking up lodgings near Namur. There was certainly plenty of work to keep him busy. Between June 1943 and April 1944, the Allied Combined Bomber Offensive (CBO), which was part of the European Strategic Bombing Campaign, made a priority of Luftwaffe targets, including aircraft factories and airfields. RAF Bomber Command missions were mainly carried out at night, while US 8th Air Force operations mostly flew by day. Up to eighteen bombing missions could be carried out over a three-month period. This wall-to-wall coverage also resulted in significant Allied aircraft losses to flak and Luftwaffe fighters. Survivors continued to parachute in increasing numbers into the Dutch and Belgian countryside.

The Comet line continued to help scores of evaders to find their way south via Paris to Spain and then Gibraltar but the pressure from the Gestapo was unrelenting. Masson was slowly but surely identifying Comet helpers in Brussels and one after another they were sent off for interrogation before consignment to concentration camps.

In the meantime, a new head of Comet operations had arrived in Paris to replace Frederick de Jongh. Jacques Le Grelle had served in the Belgian cavalry and was also very well travelled. Having visited the United States, he retained an American accent when speaking English. He also enjoyed sports, including skiing. When skiing near Osnabrück in Austria he befriended a German officer. After hostilities began, Le Grelle was made a PoW. Fortunately, the officer in charge of the camp was the same one that he had met in Austria. Le Grelle and some of his companions were given special passes that enabled them to leave the camp and make their way back to their home country. Having reached Brussels, Le Grelle decided to try to go to England and he set off south and crossed the Pyrenees. He was arrested by Spanish Guardia Civil and sent to a camp at Figueras, where he stayed for six months in appalling conditions. He was then moved to the Miranda de Ebro concentration camp. Having escaped, he reached Madrid and then found his way to Gibraltar. He arrived in England on 10 August 1942.

The Belgian military authorities in England asked Le Grelle if he would be prepared to return to the Continent. Having consented, he was put in touch with MI9. Le Grelle was sent off for specialist training but cracked his spine on a parachute jump and had to convalesce for eight months. By May 1943, however, he was on his way to Pembroke dock to catch a seaplane that would take him to Portugal. He made his way over the Pyrenees and reached Paris, where he took charge of Comet operations, based in the rue de Longchamps.

In view of the continuing pressure, the three Comet heads, d'Ursel, Le Grelle and Nothomb, decided to meet in Paris to discuss the way forward. It was reminiscent of the meeting between Dédée, Frederick de Jongh and Jean Greindl, and equally ominous. These after all were unarmed civilians fighting for survival against a sophisticated and ruthless intelligence organisation in the form of the Gestapo. They had no way of knowing how much information the authorities might have gathered about them or when to expect a knock on the door. Their only real support was the knowledge that, despite everything, the Comet line was still successfully escorting airmen, including an increasing number of Americans, to freedom, each one of them providing a significant morale boost to their comrades when they returned.

Apart from the ongoing challenges of evading the Gestapo, Antoine d'Ursel also wanted to discuss a new idea. In view of the growing number of Comet and other associated escape line helpers who had been compromised by the Gestapo and who were in hiding or on the run, he wanted to create a parallel escape line focused on them. His plan was to cross the Pyrenees and return to England so that he could discuss this idea with the British.

The others agreed to the plan and d'Ursel and Nothomb caught the train to Bayonne, accompanied by four American airmen. Then they set off for Ciboure, located on the other side of the river Nivelle from St-Jean-de-Luz. They waited in a cottage for Florentino to arrive but received a message that he was unwell with flu and would not be available to guide them. This would prove the first in a series of mishaps that would turn the night before Christmas Eve 1943 into a tragedy.

Inquiries were made and two Basque smugglers were found who were prepared to guide the group for the right price. In due course, having regained their energy from some homely cuisine, they set off up the hill, picking up the landmarks that would be familiar to the many evaders who had gone before them. Despite the disappointment of not being guided by the 'man mountain' himself, all appeared to be going to plan as they descended towards the Bidassoa river. It had rained heavily the previous night and the river was in spate. The guides would have to take great care in supporting the men as they crossed. The airmen were instructed to take off their trousers and to wrap them round their necks. One by one, the four Americans were helped across and reached the other bank, where they put their trousers back on and climbed up the far bank with one of the guides. The other guide came back across to collect Antoine d'Ursel, who by now was shivering in the cold air. D'Ursel had spent some time in the far east and had had occasional bouts of malaria. The guide began to help him across, the freezing water tearing at their legs. D'Ursel suddenly lost his footing and fell in the water, pulling the guide with him. The guide swam to the bank on the Spanish side while d'Ursel managed to grasp at the branch of a tree on the French side and painfully pulled himself out of the water. Nothomb came to his aid and dragged him shivering up the bank. He tried to persuade Antoine to go back to the farm and to try to cross another day. After all, he now had no dry clothes and little chance of getting warm. But d'Ursel was adamant: having come this far, he had no plans to turn back now – he had to get to the other side.[1]

Realising that argument was pointless, Nothomb got ready to help d'Ursel over the river again. They made their way down the bank and entered the water, feeling the force of the current against their legs. D'Ursel was holding on to the trousers around Nothomb's neck. Then they heard shots ringing out from the Spanish side of the river. It was obvious that the others had run into a Spanish patrol. The distraction was enough to cause d'Ursel to lose his footing and he fell into the water, dragging Nothomb with him. Nothomb managed to swim to the bank on the French side but there was no sign of d'Ursel. He pulled himself up on to the bank and then he heard more shots. This time he could see the muzzle flashes in the dark. The Spanish Guardia Civil were getting close. Nothomb lay low and let the silence and the dark conceal him until the danger had passed. Then he made his way back to Ciboure to break the tragic news. It was obvious to him that d'Ursel must have drowned. D'Ursel was not the only one. USAAF Second Lieutenant Jim Birch was also swept away by the current and was drowned that night.[2]

Nothomb continued to escort evaders, taking four across the border on the night of 28–29 December with the aid of Florentino, when he also met Michael Creswell. However, as Airey Neave had feared, the Gestapo net was tightening. The Gestapo had a rather vague picture of Jean-François Nothomb, as they did not know that he was also Franco. By January 1944, however, Jacques Desoubrie, alias Jean Masson, had been tipped off that airmen were coming and going from a premises in the sixteenth arrondissement, and they set up surveillance in the area.

In the meantime, Nothomb was planning to meet with Michelle Dumon, otherwise known as Lily or Michou, a petite, pretty

young woman who was determined to keep the line going, whatever the cost. She knew how to exploit her little girl looks when
the circumstances demanded. After a failed attempt at a rendezvous
in Bayonne, Nothomb and Lily met at Elvire de Greef's house in
Anglet. Lily's parents and sister had both been arrested and the
Gestapo were searching for her. Knowing that she could not survive for long in Brussels, Lily had taken a train to Paris, where she
met the newly installed Jacques Le Grelle. She had then moved
on to Bayonne. Nothomb discussed his plans to travel north to
Brussels, where he would co-ordinate plans with the new team of
Comet helpers. He then planned to go to Paris to meet Le Grelle
before liaising with Lily again to set up a new series of journeys
with evaders.

Le Grelle then accompanied Nothomb to Brussels to talk to
the Comet agents before returning to Paris on 17 January. He had
instructions from MI9 to cross the Spanish border six months after
his arrival to maintain a level of security. Unfortunately for Le
Grelle, the Gestapo unit working with Desoubrie had already gathered enough information to make an arrest and they were waiting
for him at his apartment in the rue de Longchamps when he returned
from Brussels.

Quite apart from the horrifying prospect of interrogation at the
hands of the Gestapo, Le Grelle also knew that Nothomb would
be arriving at the apartment the following day and there was nothing that he could do to warn him. When he arrived at Gestapo
headquarters, Le Grelle was greeted by a jubilant Desoubrie, who
seemed to particularly relish the shock on the faces of his victims
when they recognised him as the formerly enthusiastic Comet helper
whom they had trusted. Here he could savour the victory over those
who represented the society that he had rejected. However, even
Desoubrie did not know that by the next day he would have caught
another Comet big fish in his net.

When Nothomb left Brussels on the Paris train on Tuesday,
8 January he was accompanied by a young man called Renaud de
Pret, who wanted to travel to England. Nothomb was planning to
guide him over the Franco-Spanish border. When the train pulled

into the Gare du Nord, Nothomb had no reason to suspect that it was anything other than business as usual. They walked up the stairs to the apartment and Nothomb knocked on the door, expecting it to be opened by Le Grelle. Instead, it was opened by a man he did not recognise. Behind him, another man pulled out a gun and ordered Nothomb and de Pret to put their hands up.[3]

If he had been on his own, Nothomb might have chanced it. Shielded by the first Gestapo agent from the one with the gun and by the door, he could have made an instant dash down the stairs with a good chance of getting away. However, the young de Pret could not read his mind and was likely to have been compromised or shot. Instead, therefore, Nothomb chose to remain as calm as possible. They were taken to Gestapo headquarters, where Nothomb met a gloating Desoubrie, barely able to believe his good fortune. For Desoubrie, lightning had indeed struck twice.

Nothomb was put in an isolation cell for four days to soften him up for interrogation. When the interrogation started, Le Grelle was brought into the room, bleeding and bruised from the brutal torture that he had endured. This included the bath torture, where his head was forced under water until he was at the point of drowning, and beatings with a woven rattan whip.

Fortunately for Nothomb, his youth and Baron d'Ursel came to his rescue. As with Dédée, the Gestapo found it difficult to credit that he could be a senior leader of a sophisticated escape organisation and Nothomb was all too keen to make the most of this. He told them that he just took orders from his boss d'Ursel, who was now dead. At first, they thought he was lying but when checks were made with the border police they received confirmation that d'Ursel had indeed been found drowned in the Bidassoa river. It seemed obvious to the Gestapo that d'Ursel was the real leader and that it would not be worth interrogating Nothomb for further information. After a fortnight, he was sent to Fresnes prison and then onwards to St-Gilles prison in Brussels.

Three weeks after their meeting with Nothomb in Gibraltar, the fears of British intelligence had been realised in spades. Despite precautionary measures to minimise risk, both their man in Paris,

Le Grelle, and the linchpin of southern Comet operations, Jean-François Nothomb, were now in Gestapo hands. To make matters worse, the informer, whatever his identity, was still at large, which meant that any replacements that British intelligence sent in were liable to meet the same fate. In the meantime, pressure continued to build. Plans were moving inexorably forward for the Allied invasion of northern Europe and bombing raids were increasing exponentially.[4] It was vital for Allied plans to disrupt the movement of German reinforcements to northern France and railway systems began to take a pounding from the air in addition to disruption caused by the resistance. While it became more vital than ever to rescue a growing number of downed airmen, those same airmen were also responsible for destroying the networks that would take them south. The new plans for establishing safe areas to obviate the need for travel across France were moving well ahead. New leaders were parachuted in, including Albert Ancia to head the safe areas in Belgium and Belgian Commando officer Jean de Blommaert, code name Thomas Rutland, to head the safe areas in France. De Blommaert, sometimes called 'Big John', had the imposing physique of a paratrooper, though this was allied to a useful ability to keep one step ahead of the enemy. MI9 intelligence officers would have found it even less easy to sleep at night if they had known that these agents and their plans were being openly discussed with an eager Comet helper called Pierre Boulain, alias Jean Masson, alias Jacques Desoubrie. There were even plans to exchange substantial sums of money with Boulain to aid his activities. Who could save the MI9 agents from their inevitable fate?

The answer to that came in the diminutive form of Lily Dumon. Lily had already been involved in discussions with Comet organisers about the new plans for safe areas, including a meeting in Paris that involved the Abbé Beauvais and a young stocky man with fair hair by the name of Boulain. One thing that Lily noticed in particular about him was his polka dot tie. At the time she could not remember why it should catch her attention but afterwards she recalled something that her father had told her about Gestapo agents signalling their presence to each other with such ties.

After this meeting, Lily escorted a compromised MI9 radio operator, Charles Lafleur, to Spain. Lafleur had been discovered by a German wireless detector van, but he had fired at the soldiers coming to arrest him and jumped out of a window before making his escape. As he followed Lily and Florentino over the Pyrenees, he had a noticeable limp after damaging his leg in the fall from the window. By the time Lily returned to France, her train delayed by Allied bombing, the Gestapo net had tightened further.

When Lily tried to contact a former Comet helper, a dentist called Martine, an unknown voice on the other end of the line invited her to come on over. Feeling suspicious, Lily went to Martine's dental practice, where worried neighbours told her that the Gestapo had paid a visit and that there had been several arrests, including of Martine. Aware of the danger, Lily caught a train to Bayonne, but rather than go into hiding she decided to get to the bottom of the informer problem that was causing such disruption to the Comet line. Lily persuaded a Comet helper friend called Diane to drive her to Fresnes prison. Having approached the lions' den, with admirable audacity, Lily found a place outside the prison walls where she thought she might be heard by the inmates. She then called out to her friend Martine, asking her to identify the informer. Eventually the cry came back, 'Pierre Boulain'. For the first time, one of those who had been betrayed by Boulain, alias Jacques Desoubrie, had had the opportunity to disclose his identity to those still at large and vulnerable to his schemes.

However, Lily's behaviour did not go unnoticed by the prison authorities and she was soon approached and arrested by German sentries. Fortune favoured the brave and the prison governor was not disposed to punish such a young woman who seemed barely out of her teens and who had offered a plausible explanation that she was trying to discover what kind of food her friend might want her to bring to the prison. In due course, therefore, Lily was allowed to leave with her vital piece of intelligence.

Lily's initiative was not a moment too early. She hastened to warn Jean de Blommaert and Albert Ancia, who had a meeting scheduled with Pierre Boulain, so-called, the next day,

7 May 1944. They were planning to discuss the planned safe area camp in the Ardennes. Ancia said he would attend the meeting in any case and Lily offered to come along, though remaining out of sight. After the meeting, Ancia was reluctant to believe that Boulain was an informer, although Lily did her best to convince him. She offered to tail Boulain in case she could come up with any further evidence from his activities. However, as she followed Boulain down a street, he turned and saw her. It was obvious to Boulain that Lily knew who he really was and he began to come towards her. Lily turned and moved away and this soon developed into a chase. Lily managed to get away by running down into the Métro and jumping on to a train, hiding among the throng of passengers, while Boulain stood on the platform searching fruit-lessly for her.[5]

If Lily Dumon had been in danger before, which was certainly the case, she was now public enemy number one so far as Desoubrie and his Gestapo team were concerned. She had unmasked one of the most effective and dangerous informers working for the Nazis and could blow apart the façade behind which he and his network were concealed. Lily was brave but not naïve. She knew that she was unlikely to survive another close encounter with him and immedi-ately took a train to Bayonne. When she met Elvire de Greef, Elvire urged her to cross the border before it was too late. Lily crossed the Pyrenees and went to the British consulate in San Sebastián, where a car was organised to take her to Madrid. By now, the British authorities were extremely concerned for her safety, but it took considerable persuasion by Michael Creswell in Madrid to con-vince her that returning to France was no longer an option. Lily was offered a commission in the British Army to encourage her to continue supporting her Comet friends through intelligence sup-port from England.

Meanwhile, back in France, Ancia needed no further persuasion that the so-called Pierre Boulain was indeed a Nazi informer and traitor. With commendable courage, he organised yet another meet-ing with him, ostensibly to discuss plans for the new safe areas but in fact to give an undercover resistance executioner from the Forces

Français de l'Interieur (FFI) the opportunity to identify Boulain. After the meeting had finished, the executioner tailed Boulain. However, although someone was shot dead, it appears to have been a case of mistaken identity as Desoubrie survived the war and was arrested after the German surrender.

The Man with the Missing Finger

In 1943, the technology used by RAF Bomber Command had been improved, enabling greater precision in bombing raids.[1] In addition, the new elite Pathfinder Force flew in advance of the main bomber force to light up the targets with coloured flares. On 22 June a major raid was mounted on Krefeld in the Ruhr Valley. De Havilland Mosquitoes of the Pathfinder Force preceded the bombers to drop flares and they were followed by larger aircraft of the same force as back-up. Then came the main bomber force consisting of Stirling, Halifax, Lancaster and Wellington bombers. It was a relatively clear night as Halifax II JD244 of 51 Squadron took off at 0011 hours from RAF Snaith, near Pollington, 20 miles south of York. Heading east, the Halifax would have flown over the Humber Estuary and then over the North Sea, heading towards the Dutch coast. Although the clear night would make the target easier to identify, it was also dangerous for the bombers as they could be seen clearly by marauding Luftwaffe night fighters. Most of the designated industrial targets were hit, although there was some collateral damage to residential areas. Halifax JD244, piloted by Sergeant Fred Heathfield, was hit by flak.

Knowing that he was unable to save the aircraft, Fred made sure that all his crew members had parachuted safely. By this time, the bomber was too low for Fred to bail out himself, so he stayed with the aircraft and managed to crash-land, getting out relatively unscathed.

Heathfield made contact with a local resistance group and spent some time in the Louvain area before being moved on to Brussels. Unfortunately for Heathfield, he was put in touch with the wrong kind of group. In a supposed safe house with a certain Nurse Collet, Heathfield heard the phone go and, following a hurried conversation, the door opened and a young woman beckoned to him to come down as the 'Captain' was waiting in a car outside. Heathfield went over to a four-door Citroën Traction Avant and climbed in next to the driver, who turned to shake his hand. Fred recalled afterwards that the joint of one of his fingers was missing. The man drove on and soon stopped to pick up another supposed evader called Pollock and two Canadian airmen. The driver then took them all to an apartment block at 369 avenue A.J. Segers in one of the Brussels suburbs. When they entered the house, they were greeted by another airman, Derrick Hawthorne, whom Heathfield recognised. All seemed to be going to plan. They then went upstairs, where they found a group of five other evaders. The usual routine was for the evaders to be equipped with false papers and then taken to a hotel on the edge of the city, supposedly ready for their onward journey to the south. However, the Gestapo would then appear at the hotel and they would be arrested, which is what happened to Heathfield's group.

Heathfield and his companions were just some of the many victims of one of the most notorious Nazi collaborators of the Second World War, namely Prosper Dezitter, or the man with the missing finger. Born in Passchendaele on 19 September 1893, Dezitter fled to Canada in 1913 after being convicted of rape and sentenced to three years in prison. In Canada he served in the 1st Battalion Manitoba Regiment and was discharged in September 1918. He enlisted briefly in the RAF before returning to Belgium in 1926, where he worked as a car salesman. He was imprisoned for six years for embezzlement and marriage fraud. After the German occupation of Belgium, Dezitter joined the payroll of the Gestapo and began to adopt various personas to infiltrate resistance groups and escape lines. His fluent English enabled him to pass himself off as either a member of the RCAF or a British officer. He sometimes called himself Captain Jackson. Other names included William Herbert Call and Jack Killanine. During July and August 1943, Dezitter ran

a 'safe house' in the avenue Slegers in Brussels, which is where Fred
Heathfield and others were lured into the hands of the Gestapo. This
so-called safe house was linked to a false escape line, which convinced
victims that they were on their way to freedom. The ruse involved
accomplices such as Dezitter's mistress, Florie Dings, who would
mimic helpers from genuine escape lines such as Comet by going out
to meet evaders and accompanying them to Brussels. The arrests of
the unsuspecting evaders sometimes took place at the Gare du Midi
after they had been taken there by Dezitter or his accomplices. This
created more distance between the arrests and the collaborators. As a
result, more than seventy RAF airmen, and several USAAF airmen,
were arrested and sent to PoW camps. It is thought that about 1,000
genuine resistance fighters and escape line organisers and helpers
were sent to concentration camps or executed as a direct result of
the betrayals brought about by Dezitter.

The Belgian resistance movements as well as British intelligence
were well aware of the damage that Dezitter and other collaborators
were causing but in the murky world of occupied Europe it was
often difficult to identify the culprits before they had done their
work and moved on. Correspondence between the British security
services in August 1943 makes it clear that Prosper Dezitter was high
on the wanted list and an immediate danger to Allied personnel and
resistance organisations.[2] He is described in one letter as a 'full-
blooded and dangerous double-agent employed by the Germans in
Belgium'. The letter acknowledges Dezitter's success in his nefarious
work and notes that he 'is said to have been responsible for the arrest
and execution of many Belgians and members of the RAF'. Having
defined the threat posed by Dezitter, the correspondence moves on
to address the action that might be taken. A letter was sent to the
SOE suggesting that steps might be taken to liquidate him. SOE
replied, saying that they would be interested in arranging a 'suitable
operation' to achieve this.[3]

The head of the Belgian section of SOE, or T-Section, was Major
Hardy Amies. Having been a fashion designer before the war, Amies
was perhaps an unlikely choice for the ruthless world of counter-
espionage, but he proved to be very good at it. Amies was well aware
of the damage caused by Dezitter, and MI5 was also concerned about

Dezitter's operations. In June 1943 an SOE planning committee met to discuss what action might be taken. They devised an execution campaign that would target mostly civilian officials and collaborators like Dezitter who were working with the Nazis to damage resistance groups and escape lines. With a start date of October 1943, this execution plan was to be called Operation Ratweek.

Protocol demanded that Amies should obtain the approval of the Belgian Government in exile before the operation went ahead. However, the Belgian authorities were rife with divisions and personal agendas. Moreover, the civilian and military parts of Belgian intelligence could not agree with each other. In his history of SOE, M.R.D. Foot comments:

> Belgium took up a good deal of SOE's time and attention. There were even more quarrels than was usual among the branches of the Belgian government-in-exile ... several ministries wished to have a finger in the resistance pie and Belgium was so placed that its affairs were of intense interest to MI6, MI9 and PWE as well as to SOE.[4]

After a long hiatus, Amies was informed that the Belgian authorities could not give their approval to the Ratweek operation as 'This would involve too many difficulties.' This rather obscure phrase apparently meant that the Belgian authorities feared Nazi reprisals if the operation were to go ahead. This was a severe blow for Amies and for T-Section as other national governments in exile had given the green light for Ratweek operations to take place under their jurisdictions. It also highlighted the contrast between the obfuscation and bureaucracy of the Belgian authorities in exile and the clear-eyed determination of the resistance movements and escape lines on the ground, of which Andrée de Jongh was a shining example. Prosper Dezitter and those like him had effectively been given a reprieve.

However, Dezitter's operations did not end there. Further information about his activities emerged from an interrogation of Therese Grandjean, known as Monique. She confirmed that she had acted as an agent for Dezitter, collecting airmen from safe houses in the Liège area. She would then send a telegram to Dezitter, who would drive from Brussels to collect them. This shows how closely Dezitter's fiendish operations mimicked those of genuine escape lines such as Comet. Monique told her interrogators that she thought Dezitter was a bona fide British officer.[5]

When Micheline Aline Dumon, known as Lily or Michou, came to England in June 1944 after her close encounter with Jacques Desoubrie, she affirmed in her report that Dezitter was the most dangerous traitor still at large and that if seen or captured he ought to be disposed of on the spot.[6]

Another insight into Dezitter's activities came from Jean-George Flacon, a lieutenant in the Belgian Army. Flacon arrived in Belgium in August 1943 and came across Dezitter, who was operating under the guise of Captain Willy with an escape organisation run by Edmond Maréchal who, according to Flacon, was under the impression that Dezitter was a genuine British officer. Sometime between July and August 1943, Maréchal's wireless operator was arrested and there was little doubt that this was the work of Dezitter. Further arrests of members of the escape line followed and then Dezitter offered to arrange for Maréchal to escape to England under the pretext that he was helping him to avoid the arrests for which Dezitter himself was responsible. When Maréchal reached the rendezvous with Dezitter, Maréchal disappeared.

Apart from his work in penetrating escape organisations, Dezitter appears to have also infiltrated PoW camps, either directly or via a proxy. One such proxy was Edward Denis Pollock, who was a stool pigeon for the Germans. He gave away escape plans that were being made by his fellow prisoners in one camp and then moved to another to continue his work. On at least one occasion he was visited by a man called 'The Captain', who was none other than Prosper Dezitter.[7]

Belgian authorities in London also reported that Dezitter had managed to purloin arms dropped by Allied aircraft to help the resistance. Dezitter was also thought to have been responsible for the arrest of the commander of the Belgian Légion, Colonel Jules Bastin, who was a veteran of the First World War and served in the 1er Régiment de Chasseurs à Cheval. Bastin was sent to Gross-Rosen concentration camp, where he died.[8]

Halifax MZ630 'ZA-S' of 10 Squadron, RAF, took off from RAF Melbourne, near the village of Seton Ross in the East Riding of Yorkshire, at 2233 hours on 2 June 1944.[9] It was part of a bombing mission by 1, 4 and 8 Bomb Groups, consisting of 105 Halifax bombers, nineteen Lancasters and four Mosquitos, aimed at the vital train marshalling yards at Trappes on the western rim of Paris. The Trappes raids were part of the intensive Allied bombing offensive against railway and other transport communications that were designed to cripple the German Army's ability to reinforce its units on the north coast of France, in anticipation of the Normandy landings on D-Day. The raids would prove highly successful, reducing the operations of the French railway network by 60 per cent between 19 May and 6 June. It was this same bombing offensive that would be responsible for curtailing the work of the Comet line in moving evaders from north to south and which led to the change of plan that gave birth to Operation Marathon (see Chapter 13).

Sergeant Cliff Hallett boarded the Halifax and stowed his parachute before easing himself past the seat in the Boulton Paul mid dorsal gun turret before he could sit back in it.[10] He checked his four Browning .303 machine guns that pointed over the tailplanes and fins of the aircraft. Behind him was the navigator's astrodome and most of the crew were located in the front fuselage. His immediate concern was the mission at hand, being unaware like the rest of the crew that they were only four days away from the largest seaborne invasion in history. The other crew consisted of the pilot, Flying Officer Alexander Murray; the flight engineer, Sergeant Osselton; the wireless operator, Warrant Officer John Williams; the navigator, Flying Officer Stanley Booker; the bomb aimer, Sergeant Stokes; and the rear gunner, Sergeant Terence Gould.

Hallett heard the roar of each of the four Bristol Hercules XVI engines as they started up one after another and then rumbled together in unison as they warmed up. The pilot messaged over the intercom to check that all their systems were working, then Hallett felt the large aircraft begin to move along the perimeter track towards the take-off point, taking its place in the queue with the many other Halifax bombers heading in the same direction. Then the engines roared again as they moved down the runway, the four engines struggling to lift the aircraft, its crew and 13,000lb of bombs into the air. The aircraft then climbed to its cruising height and turned on to the course plotted by the navigator.

The raid proved to be successful, turning the railway marshalling yards into a scene of devastation, with mangled railway stock and twisted railway lines. However, there was a heavy price to be paid as fifteen Halifaxes and one Lancaster were lost. Hallett's Halifax was attacked by two German fighters, setting the two port engines and both wings on fire. The pilot gave orders to abandon the aircraft and Hallett squeezed out of his tight spot, grabbed his parachute and, having strapped it on, made his way through the escape hatch, which was opposite his turret. Neither the pilot nor the wireless operator managed to exit the aircraft before it crashed near St-André-de-l'Eure. Stokes broke a leg when jumping and had little choice other than to await capture and to be taken to hospital. Booker, Gould and Osselton managed to evade capture and were picked up by the resistance. They were given civilian clothing and transported to Paris, where they were put in a safe house. However, the Gestapo got wind of their arrival and they were arrested. As Hitler became more infuriated by the damage wreaked by Allied airmen, he decreed that any airmen caught out of uniform should be treated as spies and denied their rights as PoWs under the Geneva Convention. The two sergeants, Gould and Osselton, were therefore sent to the concentration camp of Buchenwald, where they were lucky to survive the war in the appalling conditions. Booker was sent to Stalag Luft L3, from which Allied PoWs had made the 'Great Escape' in March 1944.

Out of the seven crew of Halifax MZ630 that had set out on that summer night, two were killed, four were captured and one had remained an evader. Hallett had parachuted on to the airfield at St-André, and it was surprising that he was not spotted in such an open area. Once on the ground, he heard voices nearby and managed to get away, crawling through a field of wheat for cover, until he found somewhere to stop and rest. As dawn came, he realised that he had stopped by a German military camp. He got away quickly and found a farm, where he was taken in and given food and shelter. The local resistance chief visited the farm, interrogated Hallett and burned his RAF uniform. He then gave Hallett civilian clothes and escorted him to a house in Nonancourt, where he was taken in by the family for three weeks. Hallett, along with three other airmen, were then driven south by car and dropped at the edge of a wood. Here they were greeted by a man who introduced himself as Lucien Belgrade. He interrogated them and warned them that they had better be who they said they were. He then led them into the centre of the forest until they came upon a camp.[11]

The man who had greeted Hallett and his companions was in fact Colonel Lucien Boussa, the forest was Fréteval Forest and Cliff and his companions had just become part of Operation Marathon.

Operation Marathon

With both Prosper Dezitter and Jacques Desoubrie, alias Pierre Boulain, still at large, having evaded the attempts of British intelligence and the resistance to eliminate them, the primary organisers of the safe areas, code-named Operation Marathon, namely Jean de Blommaert, Georges d'Oultremont, Albert Ancia and Squadron Leader Lucien Boussa, remained in considerable peril. Because of his capacity to evade capture, de Blommaert was known to the Gestapo as the Fox. However, he was not so much fox as sheepdog, shepherding the lost sheep in the form of Allied airmen into pens where they would be relatively safe from marauding wolves, not least the wolf in sheep's clothing Pierre Boulain.

Operation Marathon was an extension and complement to Comet line operations. As the French railway system continued to be pounded by Allied bombers in the build-up to D-Day, ever greater efforts were made to direct airmen towards the new camps that were being set up for them. The main site in France was in the Fréteval Forest, about 100 miles south-west of Paris and between Le Mans and Orléans. The main town nearby was Châteaudun, which was also the site of a major German arsenal and air base. The Fréteval camp was code-named Sherwood and was under the command of Jean de Blommaert. The camps in Belgium were centred on the Ardennes Forest and were under the command of Albert Ancia.

Lucien Boussa declined to be dropped by parachute into France and instead travelled via Gibraltar and Madrid before crossing into

France over the Pyrenees. He met with de Blommaert in April 1944 and they put the final touches to the plan for the safe area in the Fréteval Forest. There were several challenges to be considered. How to get the evaders to the safe areas unseen, bearing in mind the presence of substantial German forces in the area? Once the men had arrived, how would they be sheltered and fed for what could be a considerable period of time until Allied forces broke out from the Normandy beachheads and advanced south and west?

The answer to both these questions depended largely as ever on the collaboration of escape lines such as Comet, local resistance organisations and the goodwill of ordinary people. Allied air drops could provide supplementary provisions, but they also risked drawing attention to the location of the camps. Having discussed the matter with Boussa in an impromptu headquarters in the village of Cloyes-sur-le-Loir, de Blommaert negotiated with local traders to supply food to the camp, bearing in mind that there was little enough to go round for the local people. He also co-ordinated with Philippe d'Albert-Lake and his American wife Virginia, who ran the Comet operation in Paris, to arrange for airmen to be escorted from Paris to Châteaudun. The basic plan was that they would take a train to Châteaudun and then walk the 15 or so miles to the camp. Sometimes they accompanied a farmer's cart and were passed off as farm workers. Timings had to be worked out as the first airmen arrived in the area before the forest camp was fully prepared. This meant that the men had to be allocated to safe houses in the locality, putting their hosts at considerable risk of reprisals should they be discovered.

While all this planning was going on, the German garrison at Châteaudun continued with its work of distributing munitions. Six 30-ton wagons would leave the compound every day on a private rail network heading for Cloyes, where the ammunition supplies would then be loaded on to trucks for distribution throughout the region. Not surprisingly, the Allies were very interested in closing down this operation and the Châteaudun munitions dump and airfield was the target for several Allied air attacks.

As the Allied air campaign continued to build, and with Châteaudun itself a high-priority target, the skies continued to rain airmen who had jumped from a range of Allied bombers and fighters that had either been hit by flak or shot up by German fighters. RAF Lancasters as well as Halifaxes and Stirlings were frequently on the scene, while USAAF was often represented by Consolidated B-24 Liberators. Occasionally, support fighters such as Supermarine Spitfires or North American P-51 Mustangs would also be brought down.

As attacks by Bomber Command on the French railway system continued, on 18–19 April 1944, 811 Lancasters and Halifaxes, accompanied by thirty-six Mosquitos, attacked four railway yards at Rouen, Juvisy, Noisy-le-Sec and Tergnier.[1] Lancaster LM361 of 9 Squadron RAF, which had flown from RAF Bardney, east of Lincoln, completed its bombing run over the station yards at Juvisy, about 18km south-east of Paris. As the Lancaster turned back for its return journey, it was hit by flak. Sergeant C.H. Martin managed to escape from the aircraft, along with Flying Officer James Arthur Smith. The other crew members, Flight Sergeant Dudley Clive Bates (RAAF), Flight Sergeant Frank Heath (wireless operator), Flight Sergeant Dennis Elver Moss (navigator) and Sergeant Ronald Wilson (flight engineer), all died in the incident. When he parachuted to the ground, Martin was lucky enough to meet with a local resistance chief and was sheltered for five weeks at Sainte-Geneviève-des-Bois. On 29 May, local gendarmes who also worked for the resistance escorted him to the Paris train, and once he arrived in the capital he was hidden at the rue Vaneau by the d'Albert-Lakes, along with other evaders.[2]

Another major series of raids took place on 20–21 April. This included five main Bomber Command attacks on transport infrastructure, including at Lens, Chambly, La Chapelle and Otignies, as well as a raid on Cologne. Lancaster W4127 of 619 Squadron took off from RAF Dunholme Lodge in Lincolnshire to bomb the railway yards at Porte de la Chapelle in northern Paris.[3] Having dropped its bomb load and as it was turning back for the return to base, the Lancaster was attacked by a Dornier Do 217N night fighter and caught fire. All but one of the crew perished in the attack. Sergeant Robert Hortie managed to escape from the aircraft, although he suffered burns. Having parachuted to the ground, he was hidden in a local farm. However, the Germans were assiduous in searching for him and approached the farm with dogs. The farmer's wife sprinkled pepper around the farmyard to put the dogs off the scent. Hortie was then moved to Marseille-en-Beauvaisis, where he stayed before being taken by Comet line helpers to Paris. On 10 June he was sent to Bellande near Fréteval and was rescued by Allied forces on 25 June.

Others were not so lucky. James Laing, pilot of a USAAF North American P-51 Mustang, was shot down while on a raid near Châteaudun.[4] Having managed to parachute safely to the ground, Laing then headed south towards Spain. He stayed with a family in Chassant, who put him in touch with the Picourt escape network and introduced him to a man called Jaques Desoubrie and his accomplice Mme Orsini. Along with a B-24 pilot called Owens, he was put on a train to Paris with all indications that he would be passed through the escape line to safety. However, when the train arrived in Paris both men were greeted by the Gestapo and arrested. After spending some weeks in Fresnes prison, they were sent to Germany and Laing ended up at Stalag Luft I at Barth.

Meanwhile, the Allies continued to pummel the Châteaudun arsenal. Carrier pigeons were dropped by Allied aircraft in small containers attached to a parachute so that the local resistance could provide information. Details were written on cigarette papers in tiny handwriting and inserted into the small canisters attached to the pigeons' legs. The value of this information is testified by the award of the Certificate of Merit of the British Empire to the resistance members who recovered the pigeons, provided the information, and sent the pigeons on their way back to England. Whether or not working on information provided by the pigeons, on 3 May Mosquito bombers dropped 900 tonnes of bombs on the Châteaudun arsenal and the detonations were said to have continued for twelve hours.

★ ★ ★

The camps that were at the heart of Operation Marathon did not just happen from one day to the next. The plan was conceived in London in conversations between Airey Neave, Jean de Blommaert, Georges d'Oultremont and Albert Ancia based on an analysis of evolving events and experiences. The fundamental challenge that faced them was the immense pressure that the Comet line was being subjected to by the Gestapo, including arrests of organisers and helpers, and the disruption of communications with southern France as Allied bombers prepared the ground for D-Day. The priority for the Allies was to disrupt as far as possible the movement of German reinforcements to northern France. The groundwork for Operation Marathon, apart from the Comet line itself and its web of contacts, was a series of alternative escape lines, allowing greater scope for moving evaders in different ways. On 15 July 1943, for example, Charles Gueulette and his radio operator Maurice Kiek parachuted into Belgium to set up Operation Felix. This independent line was designed to pass evaders from the Belgian–Dutch border to Paris, passing through a series of safe houses where they were sheltered, fed, provided with civilian clothing and issued with false identification cards. Gueulette and Kiek recruited helpers to support the line. Kiek was arrested in September while Gueulette was recalled to England, where he arrived in June 1944, having crossed the Pyrenees, and having spent a period in the Spanish concentration camp of Miranda de Ebro. The Felix line had successfully moved several evaders to safe houses in Paris, but it had also strengthened links and created new contacts that would be important as the Operation Marathon plan evolved.

Another significant player in the build-up to Marathon was Dominique Potier, code name Martin. Potier had served with the Belgian Air Force and managed to evade capture after the German invasion, making his way to Lisbon, where he found refuge in the Belgian Embassy. On 19 February 1942, he flew to England in a flying boat. There he helped to train Belgian pilots before joining the Sûreté de l'État Belge in May 1943. On the night of 14–15 July, Potier and his French Canadian radio operator Dominique Lafleur were parachuted into Suxy in the south-east of Belgium and to the east of the Ardennes forest. Potier's primary mission at this time was to enable Lysander drops and evacuations by identifying suitable landing fields. Potier and his contacts concealed evaders in the Ardennes Forest before feeding them through to the landing zones in northern France, near Reims. Potier also helped to arrange for safe houses where evaders could be sheltered and provided with civilian clothes and false papers. This also included safe houses in Paris in collaboration with the Comet line. In addition to evacuation by air, Potier and Lafleur also organised escape lines to guide evaders to either San Sebastián in north-west Spain or Barcelona in the north-east. The air evacuations took place between September and November 1943 and included the insertion of Georges d'Oultremont on 7–8 November 1943 and Lucien Dumais and Raymond Labrosse on 16–17 November on their mission to set up the Shelburne line. Potier returned to England on the same flight.

Potier wanted to discuss the constraints of Lysander operations (the aircraft was designed to carry no more than two passengers, though three were sometimes squeezed in) and the possibility of using Lockheed Hudson bombers, which could carry ten passengers, for evacuations. He was parachuted back into France on 20 December 1943 and the next day he had a meeting in Paris with de Blommaert and d'Oultremont to discuss the future of their various missions. However, Potier's luck was soon to run out. Lafleur had been transmitting to London on 28 December when the Gestapo suddenly broke in. Lafleur engaged in a gun battle and managed to escape by jumping out of a window, but the Gestapo search brought them to Potier's lodgings and he was arrested. Potier was taken initially to Fresnes prison in Brussels and then to the prison at Reims, where he was subjected to brutal interrogation under torture. One way or another, Potier fell from a second-floor window and was killed. De Blommaert maintained that he had died under torture. Lafleur escaped with d'Oultremont over the Pyrenees with the Comet line. The Gestapo continued to round up the many ordinary brave men and women who had provided safe houses for evaders. They were deported to concentration camps and many never returned.

D'Oultremont, whose mission had overlapped with that of Potier, had organised escape routes in Brittany and elsewhere. He had been recruited by Albert Greindl to help with Comet line operations in April 1942 and had accompanied evaders from Brussels to Paris. He had also been one of the team responsible for finding airmen who had been shot down over Belgium. High on the Gestapo wanted list, he was called back to England in December 1942 and crossed the Pyrenees, reaching London in January 1943. He volunteered for special duties and went on a parachute training course. He was also trained to facilitate Lysander operations and coastal evacuations with Motor Torpedo Boats (MTBs). He was flown to Compiègne in a Lysander of 161 Squadron on 7 November 1943 and proceeded to set up a series of safe houses that would enable evaders to access evasion routes via air and sea. He also ran the Possum line operations while Potier was back in England. D'Oultremont arranged the drop zone for Potier, de Blommaert and Willy Lemaitre (London) prior to their joint meeting in Paris on Christmas Day. After the arrest of Potier and the Gestapo assault on the Possum line operations, d'Oultremont met Jean-François Nothomb in Paris, when he received a message to return to England. Having been detained by the Spanish authorities at Miranda de Ebro concentration camp, d'Oultremont eventually got back to England in April 1944. He was deployed to Bayeux to help with evasion work in June 1944 and then returned to England again to join the Belgian SAS in August 1944. He served with the SAS on operations in the Netherlands and Germany.

Jean de Blommaert's activities were similar to those of d'Oultremont. During the 1940 campaign, he had served in the 2nd Regiment of the Chasseurs à Cheval. Having been wounded and then taken prisoner, he managed to escape in August 1940. He was recruited by Jean Greindl and acted as a guide for the Comet line between Brussels and Paris. In July 1943, he left Belgium accompanied by d'Oultremont and they crossed the Pyrenees to Spain with the help of a Comet guide. Once he had arrived in England, he contacted the Sûreté de l'État Belge and went on a parachute training course to prepare for deployment on special duties in occupied Europe. He was parachuted into France on 20 December 1943 along with Dominique Potier with a mission to organise air evacuations near Chartres and sea evacuations in Brittany. He returned to London via San Sebastián, Madrid and Gibraltar between January and March 1944. When he next returned to France, it would be to implement Operation Marathon.

Other missions at this time included that of Jacques Allaert (code name Allen) and Paul Sanderman (code name Simpson), who were parachuted in on 16–17 March 1944 near Saumur. First, they went to Paris, with the help of resistance workers, and then on to Belgium. Allaert was located in Brussels and Sanderman in Charleroi. Sanderman would later be arrested and deported to Buchenwald, where he died on 25 February 1945. Allaert was more fortunate. Although he was also arrested, in May 1944, and sent to Etterbeek prison, he would survive until released by the advancing Allied forces. However, although these smaller operations seemed to be snuffed out early by the Gestapo, they had the effect of keeping German military intelligence guessing at a time when they might otherwise have been congratulating themselves on their successes against the bigger escape lines such as Comet. The smaller missions also helped to rekindle relationships, creating a network of trusted helpers who would later play a significant part in establishing and maintaining the safe areas of Operation Marathon.

Albert Ancia, who was to be responsible for the Operation Marathon camps in the Ardennes, had also been directly involved in Comet line operations. Ancia had an academic background, having studied Oriental languages at the University of Louvain. He joined the student protest movement called the Groupement de Refus, which fought against German propaganda, and then joined the Belgian Légion, which later became the Secret Army. During this period, he developed a network of trusted contacts who would serve him well in Operation Marathon. Ancia's activities did not go unnoticed by the Gestapo, and he soon became a wanted man. The Comet leader Yvon Michiels arranged for Ancia to be guided to Paris by Albert Mattens. There he worked with the Comet leaders Antoine d'Ursel, Jacques Le Grelle and Jean-François Nothomb. Working under Nothomb's leadership, he guided evaders on the route from Paris to southern France. He accompanied Nothomb and d'Ursel when the latter attempted to get back to England to explain his new plan for a separate line specifically for Belgian evaders wanting to join free Belgian forces in Britain. The group also included a party of US airmen. Both d'Ursel and the US pilot Jim Burch[5] lost their lives when they slipped while crossing the Bidassoa river. Ancia found his way to Madrid and Gibraltar after a spell in the Miranda de Duero concentration camp. After he arrived in England, he spent some time in Patriotic School while the British authorities satisfied themselves that he was not an enemy plant. Having been given permission by the Sûreté de l'État Belge to train for special duties, Ancia went on a parachute training course along with other training to prepare him for deployment back to occupied Europe.

After the departure and death of d'Ursel, Michiels became head of Comet operations in Belgium. Michiels gave up his job to devote himself completely to the work of helping evaders. He was assisted by Jules Dricot, code name Jean Deltour, who by profession was an architect and who served in the Belgian 1er Regiment de Carabiniers and then undercover in the Secret Army and the resistance organisation Zero. Dricot was an effective organiser who not only recruited helpers and guides but also arranged false papers for the evaders before escorting them to Brussels and then on to Paris. On 22 January 1944, Dricot was arrested by the Gestapo and sent to Breendonk military prison, near Mechelen in Belgium. Although he suffered intensive interrogation under torture, he did not reveal anything to compromise the wide Comet network of guides and helpers in which he had played such a central role. He was then sent to Buchenwald concentration camp near Weimar in Germany. Ever resourceful and determined, Dricot attempted to escape from a prison convoy but was shot dead.[6]

There were many others who played a part in helping evaders to find safe houses and equipping them to travel under false identities, posing as ordinary citizens. Raymond Itterbeek helped thirty-four airmen to evade over the course of seventeen journeys until he was arrested on 3 January 1944, along with two evaders whom he was accompanying at the time on a train from Paris to Rumes. Although he was condemned to death and deported, he was one of the lucky ones who was relieved by the Allies before the sentence could be carried out.[7] Jacques de Struyn had a similar story to tell. Having been a member of the Belgian Légion, later the Secret Army, and then Zero, he joined Comet as a guide between Brussels and the French border. He was arrested, condemned to death and sent to Amberg prison in Bavaria, where he was later liberated by the Allies. Albert Mattens had set up a vital network of guides on both sides of the Belgian–French frontier. When he was arrested, the network collapsed. Mattens would survive the war, but his arrest showed how much damage could be done to the escape networks. With the arrest of both the first-rank leaders such as Jacques Le Grelle and Jean-François Nothomb and the death of Antoine d'Ursel, along with a swathe of second-tier organisers and guides, the Comet line effectively ceased to function in the way that it had originally been designed to do.

In view of the many arrests that took place, and the dire fate that awaited the victims, the establishment of the camps offered some relief. If the evaders were in one place and no longer in transit, they would have less requirement for safe houses prior to movement on to Brussels or from Brussels to Paris. As regards the placement of the camps, in general those evaders who were based in Paris would be moved to Fréteval Forest; those based in Brussels would be taken to the Ardennes camp; and those who were due for rescue through the Shelburne line would be taken to a camp near Rennes.

The overall leader of Operation Marathon was Jean de Blommaert, with Albert Ancia running the Ardennes operation. One of de Blommaert's responsibilities would be to persuade the leaders of the remaining escape lines to divert their evaders towards the camps. In the event, the Shelburne line organisers decided not to participate in Operation Marathon and the mainly Canadian evaders continued to try their luck with the MGBs that arrived offshore to take them off. De Blommaert had a highly able second-in-command to help him organise the camps in the shape of Lucien Boussa. Having commanded the Belgian 3/III/2 Squadron at Nivelles at the beginning of the war, when he flew Fairey Fox VI aircraft, Boussa had escaped occupied Belgium and made his way to the United Kingdom. Here he was first posted to 131 Squadron in July 1941 and then to several other squadrons before he became flight commander of 350 (BE) Squadron, taking command in December 1942. In early 1944, Boussa transferred to the SAS and walked over the Pyrenees into France. He refused to be parachuted as he had had a bad experience escaping from an aircraft. Boussa was a good man manager and played a key role in keeping the evaders busy and their morale high during the long weeks of waiting for relief by the Allies.

Fréteval

Meanwhile, Jean de Blommaert set about identifying a suitable camp in central France with the aid of the French resistance. Searching in an area south-west of Paris, they identified the forest of Fréteval as an ideal location. The nearest town was Châteaudun. The forest was about 10km long and they chose an area in the northern end. The first stage of the operation was to house the airmen in farms in the area, drawing on contacts that had been developed previously. De Blommaert and Boussa worked effectively together to make the arrangements for setting up and supplying the camps, the first of which was opened on 6 June 1944, D-Day. The logistical operation included building huts and camp beds and arranging a regular supply of food, including essentials such as bread, milk, eggs, meat and vegetables and fruit. Coffee and cigarettes were also high priorities to help relieve the boredom of the long wait.[8] The challenge was to make all these arrangements without attracting the attention of the Germans. Much depended on the loyalty of local people, who recognised when the resistance were active in the area and did their best to cover for them. Supplying the camps was a challenge in view of the restrictions that were part of daily life in occupied France and Belgium. It was remarkable that the daily supply of food, including live animals, took place daily without attracting undue attention. Some supplies were dropped by air. One of the greatest dangers was that people might be followed into the camps, and to reduce the risk the resistance kept a watch on the forest perimeter to make sure that no one entered except the limited number who provided essential services.

Ardennes

The success of the camps was due in large part to a combination of loyal local people who were prepared to risk their freedom and their lives to contribute to the fight against oppression and some key leaders who demonstrated both courage and organisational skills. Some of the local helpers made exceptional efforts despite the danger of heavy repercussions if discovered. Vincent Wuyts and his wife had a house in the centre of the village of Beffe, near the church, which became a major staging post for evaders. His efforts were recognised after the war with the award of the Croix de Chevalier de l'Ordre Léopold with palm, the Croix de Guerre with palm, the US Medal of Freedom and the British King's Medal.[9]

Emile Roiseux was a highly active guide who had helped evaders from October 1943 onwards, guiding them from Brussels to the French frontier. He was helped in this work by his wife, Catherine Ryckaert. Roiseux showed remarkable presence of mind in January 1944 when he was called to a rendezvous, only to find the Gestapo waiting for him. Without missing a beat, he announced that he was the plumber who had been called to check a fault in the cistern. Having checked the cistern and announced that it was *kaput*, he then left, leaving the Gestapo to continue waiting for their suspect. Roiseux then hurried off to warn his fellow resistance members of the Gestapo trap. Roiseux's major contribution to Operation Marathon was the Camp at Porcheresse, east of Bastogne. Along with about six helpers, he set up and organised the camp, arranged for provisions and provided shelter for more than twenty evaders.[10]

Another significant contributor to the success of the camps was Georges Arnould. Arnould had been a Comet line helper, having previously served in the 1er Regiment de Carabiniers. In the six months between 26 July 1943 and 6 January 1944, Arnould helped twenty-seven airmen to evade through the Comet line. Jean Serment recruited Arnould to establish a camp in the Ardennes and he adapted seamlessly to his new role. With the help of a local gamekeeper, he found a suitable location in the forest of Luchy, near Acremont. He then set about building a cabin, which was constructed without nails to avoid the sound of hammering. Twenty-eight evaders moved into the camp on 28 August 1944, most of whom were Americans. Arnould impressed everyone with his quiet efficiency and dedication in running the camp and providing for the evaders. His helpers included Eugene Gerard, who provided transport and provisions; Renee Soroge and his wife Lucie Wavreille, who supplied the evaders with their daily bread; Josue Duroy, the gamekeeper, who provided a range of practical assistance; and the abbot Jules Massin.[11]

Among the American airmen in the group, the most senior was Captain Joseph Lincoln, who took responsibility for discipline. He had been the pilot of a B-17 bomber that had made a forced landing in France on 24 April 1944. Flight Lieutenant Samuel Schleichkorn had been the pilot of a Consolidated B-24 Liberator of USAAF that had taken part in a 455-bomber raid on Zwickau and Oschersbelen on 12 April 1944.[12] Two crew had died, three had been taken prisoner and five, including Schleichkorn, had managed to escape. The Secret Army provided help and they found their way to the camp.

After the war, Georges Arnould was awarded the Croix de Chevalier de l'Ordre de Léopold with palm and Croix de Guerre with palm. He received high praise from Comet leaders Albert Ancia and Albert Mattens for his quiet devotion to duty and courage.

While the camps continued to develop, Gaston Matthys still held out in Brussels as head of the Comet line. However, the Gestapo ring was closing. German intelligence was working methodically to narrow down Matthys' real identity and location, having ploughed through a host of pseudonyms. Wisely, Matthys no longer used his home residence and he had also abandoned his office. On 7 August 1944, the Gestapo turned up at his office to arrest him, only to find that he was not there. On 10 August, they arrived at his home. Again, the bird had flown. Even though the Germans had set up a tight cordon around the house, Matthys' wife managed to escape, using a pre-arranged plan. As the Gestapo circulated photographs of him, Matthys left Brussels with Albert Ancia and the two of them rode on bicycles into the countryside and made their way to the Ardennes. However, their troubles were not over. Having sought shelter in the village of Villance, they woke the next morning to discover that it had been surrounded. Fortunately, the German soldiers who checked their papers were not on the same wavelength as the Gestapo in Brussels and the two men were allowed to go on their way.

The camp at La Cornette was managed by Germain Servais, who had in turn been recruited by Abbé Jerome. An energetic guide who had helped many evaders to reach the camps, Abbé Jerome walked or cycled many miles, while also acting as a liaison or supplying provisions. He was helped by Abbé Jules Massin from the seminary at Reims. Airmen began to arrive at La Cornette on 29 August 1944, but they soon became impatient to join the Allied forces, whose approach was signalled by the sound of gunfire in the distance. One airman decided to try his luck but, after being spotted by a German soldier who fired at him, and barely escaping with his life, he returned to the camp to advise his fellow evaders against trying the same thing. Eventually, however, a small American unit arrived in the area consisting of a lieutenant and about twenty soldiers. As they approached the camp, the evaders kept their heads down, fearing they might be Germans, but were soon relieved to discover that they had been liberated. Chesterfield and Camel cigarettes were put between smiling lips and the evaders had a last meal before leaving the camp. They were escorted to Paris by Matthys, including eleven airmen of USAAF, four from the RAF, three from the RCAF and two from the RAAF.[13]

Further east was Bohan camp, the only one of the Marathon camps located in Luxembourg. This was managed by Herbert Renault, a veteran of the twenty-eight-day campaign who had been recruited into the Comet line in 1943. Renault had initially helped to set up the camp at Villance before moving on to Bohan, where he had his home and where he could call on reliable contacts to assist with the setting up and maintenance. Renault was assisted by Oscar Laplang, Alexis Heury and Marius Heury, among others. A large hut was positioned near a spring. It was far enough from the nearest habitation to be secure but also close enough to make resupply on foot manageable. As ever, the security of the camp depended on the loyalty of the few in the area who knew of its location. Also nearby was a mill with a farm attached that could be used to store provisions or temporarily conceal evaders.[14]

On 5 August, ten airmen arrived at the camp, escorted by Abbé Jerome. In due course, they were joined by twenty-eight additional airmen who had been transferred from the other camps and by four Comet guides, namely Jacques Bolle, Angele Lenders, Yvonne Bienfait and Henri Nys.

As the Allies advanced, local villagers advised the evaders that American units were approaching. As the Germans had blown up the bridge during their retreat, the airmen had to wade across the river to greet their liberators. An American scout car arrived, and K-rations were distributed to the evaders before they were taken to their local headquarters, where the evaders were interrogated. They were then sent further back to the central command headquarters, where they were interrogated once again. The evaders were then put on a truck that took them to Paris, travelling through villages full of celebrating local people. Once they had arrived in Paris, they were taken to the Hotel Maurice, where they stayed for up to four days before being flown to London. They were interrogated by the Air Ministry and then given four weeks' leave before returning to their units.

14

Adieu Paris

The transition that the ever-adaptable Comet line made from evasion to the south and the Spanish border, to refuge within France and Belgium, is no better exemplified than by the experience of Philippe and Virginia d'Albert-Lake. Virginia wrote a detailed diary of the events surrounding her work for the Comet line and her arrest and experiences in German concentration camps, on which the information in this chapter is based.[1] Having embraced the work of custodians of a safe house in Paris, they performed an agile pivot supplying the camp at Fréteval with Allied evaders.

Virginia Roush was an elegant young American who had visited France as a schoolteacher in 1936 and fallen in love with Philippe d'Albert-Lake, whose double-barrelled name indicated a French father and English mother. They were married the next year. Although they lived mostly in Paris, they also acquired a cottage in the quiet village of Nesles, north of Paris. It was during a visit to the cottage in autumn 1943 that they were invited to dinner by the local baker, only to find his dining room full of young men who turned out to be downed airmen. The baker was planning to pass them on to the Comet line to arrange their journey south and the d'Albert-Lakes realised that they needed to be involved. They soon became enthusiastic members of Comet and highly valuable ones, too. Like Elsie Maréchal, as a native English speaker and familiar with American slang, Virginia was able to question new evaders to check that they were not German spies. However, her American accent also left her exposed to suspicion if she were to be questioned by the authorities. Having been briefed on the methods used by the Comet line, Virginia and Philippe plunged enthusiastically into their dangerous work of meeting, housing and feeding evaders passing through Paris en route to the south.

Their usual routine was to pick up evaders from the Gare du Nord and then take them on a guided tour of Paris. While in the city, the d'Albert-Lakes and their helpers followed the Comet guidelines, which included walking together in pairs, with one pair feigning no knowledge of the others. Female guides would act as if on intimate terms with their ward on the streets but this would not be the case in the Métro or on trains, where they would remain separate. As the evaders would almost invariably have little or no French, they were given German-language magazines and newspapers to help ward off any friendly inquiries from the locals. The Comet guides would always remain in visual contact with the evaders so as to provide reassurance and to be able to intervene in any compromising situations if necessary.

Although initially the evaders were housed in a studio flat acquired by the d'Albert-Lakes to avoid attracting attention to their own apartment, in due course they began to take them to a house in a village outside the city where they were less likely to attract unwelcome attention. Here they would stay in relative safety while arrangements were made to provide them with false identity papers and tickets for the journey south.

Jean de Blommaert liaised with the d'Albert-Lakes in Paris before leaving to organise the Fréteval camp. He left Philippe in charge of the Paris Comet line operations. Allied bombing activity was expanding and along with the increased number of aircraft came a growing number of downed airmen seeking to evade. As the Paris operation came under greater pressure, the d'Albert-Lakes could no longer afford to take the men out of Paris, and they were all housed in the studio flat. Hungry young men obviously needed regular supplies of food and Virginia would often go out to find supplies, which she would carry in her bicycle basket, hoping that she would not be stopped and asked whom the food was for. Due to rationing, some of the supplies had to be obtained on the black market.

When the fateful day of the Allied invasion of Normandy finally arrived, communications out of Paris all but ceased. It was time to action Plan B and find a way of escorting the evaders to the Fréteval Forest camp. The only train that they could find heading in the south-westerly direction of Châteaudun and Fréteval went as far as Dourdan, 30km outside Paris on the edge of the Parc Naturel de la Haute Vallée de Charente. They would have to cover the remaining 90km under their own steam. Virginia and Philippe booked ten evaders on to the train and then returned to the studio to collect their bicycles, having arranged a rendezvous in a forest near Dourdan. Once they had found the evaders, they had lunch before setting off on the long journey. Walking through open country, it began to rain heavily and they were all drenched. When they eventually reached a village, they received a frosty reception as the inhabitants had already suffered German reprisals for having sheltered evaders. Cold, wet and hungry, they moved on until they came to another village adjacent to a farm. Here they had better luck and the farmer provided them with hot soup and bread and a place to sleep.

They agreed that Virginia should go on ahead the next morning to make initial contact with the resistance and warn them of the arrival of the men. She would also make inquiries about transport to come and pick up the tired and foot-sore evaders from the farm. Virginia and Philippe set off the next morning and reached Châteaudun at five o'clock in the afternoon. They noticed that the station and railway had been bombed and that the town was full of German soldiers. They made their way to a grocer, where they gave an agreed password and were shown to a flat by a member of the resistance. They were given a meal by the resistance member in his flat with his wife and small children before being shown to a farm owned by the Merets family, where they spent the night in a hayloft with other members of the resistance. The next morning, the resistance produced a horse and wagon to collect the men. Virginia and a resistance member called Henri set off with the wagon, which was driven by Jean Merets, while Philippe went off to Bellande to make arrangements with Jean de Blommaert for the reception of the evaders.

As Virginia and Henri cycled along with the wagon, the air filled with the sound of Flying Fortresses overhead, while German trucks pulled over to the side as a precaution. Eventually, they reached the evaders and the ever-resourceful Virginia shared out a picnic of sandwiches, chicken, hardboiled eggs and beer to the waiting men. Then they set off again, with the men on board the wagon, and Virginia and one of the American airmen called Al riding bicycles along with Henri. They took a circuitous route, designed to reduce the risk of running into a German patrol. When they were about 8 miles from Châteaudun, Henri left them to attend another rendezvous. As they approached the main road near the village of Le Plessis, Virginia could see Châteaudun ahead on a hill. They bicycled on and then paused to wait for the wagon to catch up. As they waited, a large black car turned into their road from the main highway. Virginia and Al pulled their bicycles over to the side to let the car pass, but it stopped next to them and they could see that it contained three Feldgendarmerie. An unidentified source says that the policemen had just stopped initially to ask the way and became suspicious when they heard Virginia's accent. Whatever the reason, one of the policemen ordered them to get off their bicycles and they then got out of the car. They asked to see their identity papers and, as a policeman checked Virginia's papers, he asked what she was doing in the area as her papers indicated that she was resident in Paris, and he also noted that she had an American accent. She explained that she was French by marriage and had permission to leave the Paris area.

In her diary, Virginia describes the emotions that overwhelmed her at that moment. Although it was a sunny day, everything seemed suddenly dark. Grasping at the remaining hope of freedom, Virginia began to move on, but the policeman barked at her to stay where she was before he began to question Al. Despite his papers stating that he was French, it soon became clear that Al could not speak a word of his supposedly native language. It did not take the policeman long to guess that Al was an American as well.

While this was going on, Virginia could see that the wagon had come to a halt about 30 yards up the road and that the evaders were surreptitiously climbing out of the back and disappearing into the undergrowth. Then the policeman turned back to her and took her handbag before searching through the contents. Virginia's heart fell even further when she realised that she had left a piece of notepaper in the bag with the names and addresses of the resistance contacts at Châteaudun. If this was discovered, it would mean certain arrest for the resistance workers she had met recently and their wives and young children. The policeman then closed the bag and gave it back to her before turning to search Al. Virginia covered the bag with her coat and reached inside to grasp the notepaper, which she then tore into pieces, stuffing them in the coat pocket. They were told to get into the car and were then driven off to the Feldgendarmerie headquarters in Châteaudun. Once inside the building, while the exuberant policeman reported their arrest to the staff at the desk, Virginia took the opportunity to put the bits of notepaper in her mouth and, with considerable difficulty, chewed and swallowed them. The policeman then came over and took Virginia's handbag, which he emptied on to the desk. He began to search through the items with signs of ever-increasing concern. He was obviously trying to find the notepaper that he had seen earlier. Then he went out to the car to search there. When he came back in, he noticed a small piece of notepaper that Virginia had inadvertently dropped on the floor. He picked it up and came over to her. When asked, she confirmed that she had eaten the notes. It was a small moment of victory in this dark hour. There was not much the policeman could do without advertising his own mistake for having given the handbag with the notepaper in it back to Virginia at the initial stop and search.

Virginia was then strip-searched before being taken in a car to the prison at Chartres. She was led down to a dark and dank cell to await her fate at the hands of the Gestapo. In due course, she was escorted to Gestapo headquarters in the rue des Saussaies, where she was questioned once again about the contents of her handbag. She and Al were then taken to Fresnes prison, where she was put in a shared cell. During her time at Fresnes, Virginia was interrogated twice by the Gestapo at the rue des Saussaies but she was determined not to give anything away, especially when she witnessed the condition of some of the men and women who had been tortured. Fortunately for her, she was not subjected to torture herself. On 1 August, she was taken to Romainville prison, which was a staging post for prisoners en route to Germany. She and her fellow inmates were tantalised by the sound of Allied artillery in the distance and dared to hope that their onward journey might be curtailed by the arrival of the Allies or made impossible by bombed railways or bridges. On 15 August, with the Allies only 60km away, they were put on buses and taken to a suburban railway station that had escaped the Allied bombers. In the hot August weather, they were then crammed into wagons before the train set off for Berlin. Here they were met by shouting SS guards and taken on to Ravensbrück concentration camp, which was about 90km north of the city.

On 11 September, Virginia and her companions were packed into box cars for a journey to Stalag IV-D at Torgau. When they reached the camp, they came across French PoWs who told them that the Allies had crossed the border into Germany. Once again, the flames of hope were kindled and the psychological and physical battle for survival continued. However, Virginia and other inmates were horrified to discover that Torgau was also a munitions factory. She and many others could not countenance making munitions that would be used to kill Allied soldiers. Those who protested were told by the camp commandant that they must return to Ravensbrück. This was a hard choice to make because the living conditions were considerably better at Torgau.

By the first week of October, they were back again on familiar territory at Ravensbrück and yet it seemed even worse than before. The anticipation of liberation by the Allies sharpened the need for survival at all costs, even as they were bullied and intimidated by camp guards and as their physical and psychological endurance was tested to the limit. In mid-October, Virginia and others were taken to Königsberg before returning to Ravensbrück at the beginning of February 1945. At the end of that month, Virginia was informed that she could leave and was taken to a Red Cross camp near Lake Constance, where prisoner exchanges were organised. Soon she was on the way to Liebenau, an ex-Catholic institution that was used to house American and British women. On 27 May 1945, Virginia arrived in Paris. Almost the first news she heard was that her mother had died on the eve of her liberation. Philippe had escaped to England, where he had joined the Free French forces.

15

The Convoy

The Allied advance into the Low Countries followed the rout of German armed forces after their near encirclement at Falaise. Here they had been caught between the First Canadian Army, part of the 21st Army Group, advancing from the north, and the US 1st Army advancing from the south. This episode resulted from Hitler's instructions, against the advice of his senior commanders, to thrust Army Group B under Field Marshal Gunther von Kluge towards Mortain, where elements of the US Army stubbornly refused to be shifted. As the Allied ring began to close, German forces tried desperately to escape. While some got away, despite being pounded and strafed, around 50,000 were taken prisoner, and 500 tanks and assault guns were lost. It marked a decisive defeat for German forces in Normandy and the end of Operation Overlord.

German forces retreated behind the Seine and the Allies relieved Paris. Three Allied armies then advanced eastwards, with the British 21st Army on the left flank, dealing with the Channel ports. In the centre was the 12th Army Group, commanded by General Omar Bradley, and in the south was the 6th Army Group under Lieutenant General Jacob L. Devers. Operation Dragoon, the Allied landings in the south of France, had taken place on 15 August and soon achieved its objectives. As the Allies advanced eastwards, their supply lines became ever more stretched as they were still largely dependent on the Normandy ports. This along with increased

German resistance meant that the advance began to slow. As the German forces retreated, on the other hand, their supply lines became shorter. The capture of the major port of Antwerp was a priority so that supplies could be brought closer to the Allied front line. The 2nd Canadian Army crossed the border into Belgium on 2 September and on the same day General Brian Horrocks ordered the British Guards Armoured Division to drive to Brussels. They covered over 100km and arrived in the city on 3 September to be greeted by surprised and jubilant citizens. Antwerp finally fell on 4 September to the 11th Armoured Division, and partly due to the valiant efforts of the Belgian resistance, which thwarted German attempts to sabotage the port, Antwerp was almost entirely intact and would prove to be a vital Allied supply point. The Battle of the Scheldt[1] was fought from October to clear the approach to the port for shipping. On 4 September the 1st Infantry Brigade of the Free Belgian Forces, or Brigade Piron, arrived in Brussels to a rapturous welcome. They were congratulated by General Montgomery when he visited the city. He complimented them on their conduct and bravery during the Normandy campaign. On 8 September the Belgian Government in exile under Hubert Pierlot returned to Brussels to restore free democratic government.

The US 1st Army moved into areas south of Brussels and a line was formed south of Liège that extended through the Ardennes and into Luxembourg. The Ardennes was designated as a quiet area where units could be rested. However, as in June 1940, the Ardennes would prove to be far from quiet and would once again become the scene of a fateful episode in the war.[2]

The advance eastwards and the breakout from Normandy was accompanied by several special operations missions, many of which involved the British Army's newest regiment, the Special Air Service (SAS). Formed in North Africa in 1941 by David Stirling, it had soon earned the approval of Winston Churchill and was set fair to continue its daring exploits as the Allies advanced through Italy and in north-west Europe. The SAS performed at its best when given free rein to operate behind enemy lines, striking targets of opportunity with devastating force, and then withdrawing before the enemy

knew what had hit them. The SAS attracted individualists and mav-
ericks across all ranks and seniority was not so much conferred as
earned. These were men who could barely see a rule without breaking it. In the warm embrace of friendly forces, however, they lost
their edge and their raison d'être.

During the Allied invasion of occupied Europe, the role of the
SAS, often working with local resistance and maquis, was to disrupt
German communications and delay the movement of reinforcements. The 1st SAS Regiment was deployed during Operation
Overlord, while 2nd SAS remained in Scotland, awaiting further
orders. The 4th SAS Battalion (Free French) were landed by gliders
near Vannes in Brittany, where they teamed up with local resistance
fighters. However, they were heavily engaged by German forces in
the area and forced to disperse. Many were captured and executed
under the notorious Commando Order,[3] issued by Hitler.

Having chafed at the bit, 2nd SAS parachuted a reconnaissance
party into southern Normandy on 19 July to gather intelligence.
However, due to the rapidly changing situation on the front line,
their mission was nullified by the presence of advancing Allied
forces. This pattern was repeated when the main force of 2nd
SAS arrived in Normandy and engaged in Operation Dunhill.
This mission was designed to frustrate German forces in advance
of Operation Cobra, the American breakout from Normandy.
However, the American advance was so rapid that the SAS squadrons were soon overtaken. One such unit was commanded by
Major Anthony Greville-Bell, who was in almost every sense the
epitome of an SAS officer. Greville-Bell had led a successful SAS
operation in northern Italy in September 1942 called Operation
Speedwell. Having parachuted into the Apennines, the SAS soldiers set about disrupting German rail communications in order
to hinder their reinforcements heading south to counter the Allied
advance in Italy. They blew up three trains, among other damage,
before heading south to rejoin friendly forces. Greville-Bell had
continued with the mission despite having broken two ribs when
he landed in a tree during the initial jump.[4] It was this officer and
his squadron that Airey Neave found parked at the Hotel Moderne

in Le Mans when he arrived to organise a rescue mission to retrieve the evaders in Fréteval Forest.

Neave's movements, as he set out to personally lead the relief effort to the camps, mirrored the progress of the Allied armies. Although ostensibly attached to 21st Army Group Headquarters as a General Staff Officer (Intelligence), Neave was determined to conduct his own operation in the field and was accompanied by a small staff. These included a French liaison officer, Capitaine Gilles Lefort, and American Major James Thornton of IS9 (WEA). Part of Neave's difficulty was that, even though there were four intelligence field sections (one British, one Canadian and two American), which were equipped with Jeeps, they did not have the firepower to operate independently or carry out rescue missions unassisted. His chances of carrying out a rescue effort depended therefore either on the Allied advance pushing the Germans away from the Châteaudun and Fréteval Forest area or on being provided with enough transport and armed and armoured support to carry out the mission.[5]

Neave waited for three weeks for a breakthrough and, finally, at the beginning of August US forces broke through German lines at St-Lô, south-west of Bayeux, and Avranches, near Mont St Michel. Neave took advantage of the new situation and set off for Rennes along roads littered with the detritus of the German retreat. However, when he arrived he found that the evaders in the area had already departed.

As General Patton's 3rd Army advanced eastwards towards Paris, Neave could be fairly confident that the line of march would take him towards the Fréteval Forest. After being delayed by the German counter-attack at Mortain, Neave reached Le Mans on 10 August but here his hopes of continuing to ride in the slipstream of the American advance were dashed. Patton had been ordered to divert his force northwards towards Alençon in order to close the Falaise Gap, which would prove to be the decisive moment in the Battle of Normandy. Despite Neave's personal plea to the American XV Corps who were based near Le Mans, the Americans were unwilling to commit transport to a foray into enemy-held territory without the support of at least light tanks and these they could not spare. However, the dark clouds of despair were quickly cleared when Neave returned to his hotel to find a squadron of heavily armed SAS Jeeps sitting in the car park.[6]

In his own account, Neave tells how he was pulled in different directions as he sought unsuccessfully to obtain transport and armoured support from the local American forces; searched for transport with the French resistance in Le Mans; and received visits from both Lucien Boussa and Jean de Blommaert, who pressured him to take action immediately to rescue the forest-dwelling evaders.[7]

The presence of the SAS at least provided Neave with considerable fire support as well as communications via their radio net with London. The French resistance worked assiduously to fulfil the requirement for coaches to bring the evaders back and found some abandoned German Army buses that, with a considerable amount of maintenance, could be made serviceable. While Boussa and de Blommaert continued to impress on him the urgency of the situation, Neave battled with the knowledge that, while he was sure the SAS could give a good account of themselves if they all ran into trouble, the evaders would be in soft-skin vehicles and would be highly vulnerable to direct fire or would be likely to disperse into the countryside, defeating the whole object of the exercise.

As the resistance worked on repairing the vehicles, Neave got together with his American and French assistants, Thornton and Lefort, along with the resistance leaders and the SAS officers to devise a plan. He also sent one of his staff, Captain Peter Barker, to the forest with an SAS escort to reassure the evaders that help was on its way. A rendezvous was agreed on the edge of the forest between Vendôme and Cloyes where the evaders could gather to await transport. Once he had news from the resistance that all the coaches were in working order and ready to go, Neave gave the order for the rescue to take place the following morning. They set off at 8 a.m. with an escort of SAS Jeeps and drove through the forest to the rendezvous point. There they saw Lucien Boussa and Jean de Blommaert with a crowd of cheering men. They all boarded the coaches and set off again at the best speed possible. Once they reached Le Mans, the men were driven to an old French Army base, where they found a meal awaiting them. Afterwards, they were loaded on to US Army trucks and taken to a US base for debriefing. In due course, they were routed onwards back to their bases in England. A total of 132 evaders, including Americans, British, New Zealanders and Canadians, had been rescued.[8]

For Neave and the rest of IS-9 (WEA), the rescue operations continued. Under Plan Endor, the IS-9 operatives would debrief the PoWs released from German camps. Neave first set up a headquarters in Paris at the Hotel Windsor,[9] where he was able to identify some of the Comet line helpers and those from other escape lines. Neave's colleague Jimmy Langley first moved to Rambouillet with his staff on 24 August. They took the earliest opportunity to drive into Paris with a plan to find helpers and any remaining evaders still in hiding and in the hope of rescuing them from any reprisals from the departing Germans.[10] When Langley arrived in the city, he went straight to the house where he himself had been hidden as an evader years before. The next day Langley set up his headquarters at the Hotel Maurice in the rue de Rivoli and took time off to watch the procession as General de Gaulle marched from the Arc de Triomphe to the cathedral of Notre Dame. After the liberation of Brussels, Langley moved there to carry out the same work, finding several evaders at the Hotel Metropole. Langley noted that there were pitifully few escape line helpers and organisers who had returned from the concentration camps, although he visited some in hospital.[11]

In the meantime, not all was going well with the Allied advance. Operation Market Garden, devised by General Bernard Montgomery to fast forward to the end of the war, met unexpectedly fierce opposition that underscored the over-optimistic planning. Despite the valiant efforts of all the Allied units that were involved, notably the 1st British Airborne Division, US 101st Airborne Division and 82nd Airborne Division, Polish 1st Independent Parachute Brigade and XXX Corps, the main armoured force was not able to get through to the bridge at Arnhem being held tenaciously by British paratroopers. Allied efforts now turned to extracting the remnants of the force north of the river Rhine. The first major evacuation, named Operation Berlin, took place on 25 September. General Urquhart arranged for normal radio communications to continue and for artillery to carry on firing so as not to signal any change to the Germans. The wounded and medical orderlies were given weapons to keep up sporadic firing from the perimeter of the Hortensen Hotel, where the remaining Allied defence was centred. Then, in a movement that Urquhart compared to the collapse of a paper bag, the main body of men peeled off from the front and passed along the lines before making their way towards the river following a route signalled by white tape.[12] At the river they were met by British and Canadian engineers manning boats who ferried them across the river. Some 2,400 men were rescued during the night and the operation continued until daylight.

Despite the success of the operation, a substantial number of Allied troops remained in hiding in German-occupied territory. They were distributed in villages around the area by the Dutch resistance. Many were held in Ede courtesy of the resistance led by Bill Wildboer but there were so many that it was difficult to keep them concealed from the Germans. MI9 had already worked closely with the Dutch resistance to spirit out Allied airmen who had been shot down over the Netherlands. Dick Kragt had been parachuted into the Netherlands in June 1943 and, along with his associate Joop Pillar, helped evaders to get to Brussels, where they were taken up by the Comet line and accompanied south to the Spanish border. This meant that MI9 already had contacts and experience of evacuation that it could draw on in the post-operation Market Garden evacuation. Airey Neave reached Nijmegen in October 1944, where he was joined by Major Hugh Fraser of the SAS. The organisation of the soldiers in safe houses was co-ordinated by Piet Kruijiff of the Dutch resistance.

Among the evaders north of the river were Major Digby Tatham-Warter, who had escaped from captivity after the Arnhem bridge operation, and Brigadier David Lathbury. Tatham-Warter had arranged with Sadi Kirschen of the Belgian SAS for the supply of weapons for the soldiers so that they could support a potential

Allied advance. They were in touch with the Dutch resistance at Ede. When it became clear that there would be no further advance by the Allies, Lieutenant Colonel David Dobie crossed the river from north to south to make arrangements for a rescue operation. A section of the river near Renkum was selected for the crossing, which was carried out with boats supplied by the British Royal Engineers and Royal Canadian Engineers. They were supported by men of the US 506th Parachute Infantry Regiment. Despite the presence of German machine gun emplacements about 500m away, the operation was successful, and the evaders reached the south side and were met by Airey Neave and his staff before they were routed back to England.

As many evaders still remained on the north side, a second similar operation code-named Pegasus II was organised. This time, however, a series of misjudgements mixed with bad luck compromised the operation. The site for the crossing was about 4km east of the previous crossing point and the date was set for 18 November. It was hoped that up to 160 men could get across during the night. However, the evaders had to walk nearly 25km to reach the site and find their way round restricted areas controlled by the Germans. The groups of evaders became separated and one group, while attempting a short-cut, ran into a German patrol that opened fire, killing several evaders. Now that they had been alerted, the Germans carried out intensive searches, resulting in the death or capture of several Dutch resistance guides. After this, no further attempts were made to organise mass evacuations, although small groups continued to attempt to get across the river.

If Arnhem was a bridge too far, the Ardennes was a forest too thin. This does not refer to the density of the trees but to the defences that the Americans had placed there. US commanders regarded it as a low-priority area where tired troops who had survived tough battles elsewhere could recuperate. It is not clear why it did not occur to US intelligence that, if the Ardennes had been the route of choice for the German Panzers in 1940, it might be again. Allied intelligence was partly based on an analysis of the likely decisions of Field Marshal Rundstedt, a general known for caution and deliberation.

However, the plan to mount an audacious counterstrike towards the river Meuse and Antwerp beyond was not Rundstedt's brainchild but Adolf Hitler's. Against the reservations expressed by his most senior generals, including Heinz Guderian, leader of the Panzer blitzkrieg in 1940, Hitler was determined that his plan to drive a wedge between the Allied forces and reach the vital port of Antwerp would work.

J.M. Langley of IS9 claims that plans were being made to retrieve and debrief evaders well in advance of a possible clash in the Ardennes. Whatever one might say about the misreading of the situation by the intelligence community, their attempts to identify the location of the Sixth Panzer Army under Sepp Dietrich were resolved quickly on 16 November when its tanks appeared in front of the thinly extended American defences and were soon supported by the Fifth Panzer Army under General Hasso von Manteuffel. The Germans went on to besiege Bastogne, causing General Patton to divert his thrust in the south to come to the aid of the American garrison. Eventually, the tide was turned, at huge cost in American and German lives, and the status quo resumed.

By 7 March 1945, the US 9th Armoured Division had reached the river Rhine. A task force that approached the town of Remagen included C Troop of the 89th Reconnaissance Squadron. When the squadron scouts climbed a hill overlooking the river, they were amazed to see the Ludendorff Bridge still intact and German forces crossing to their own side. This was one of the three remaining bridges across the Rhine that were still intact, though all had been made ready for demolition. Company A, 14th Tank Battalion, was immediately despatched to drive the remaining defenders from the approach to the bridge. US tanks engaged German flak guns on the far side of the river that were firing on the approaching American units. A reconnaissance platoon then ran across the bridge, while soldiers cut wires to the demolition charges and threw the charges themselves into the river. US forces rapidly took advantage of the situation and established a bridgehead on the German side of the river. Meanwhile, the Germans tried unsuccessfully to destroy the bridge with artillery, aircraft and V2 rockets.

This unscheduled advance into Germany was two weeks ahead of Operation Plunder. The 21st Army Group under Field Marshal Montgomery planned to cross the Rhine at Rees, Wesel and south of the river Lippe. This was to be carried out by the British 2nd Army under Lieutenant General Miles Dempsey and the US 9th Army under General William H. Simpson. The operation was supported by Operation Varsity and Operation Archway, in which the SAS crossed the Rhine in amphibious vehicles, taking their heavily armed Jeeps. In a separate operation, the US 3rd Army under General Patton crossed the Rhine at Nierstein.

With Allied armies now at large in Germany, it was just a matter of time until the incumbents of the PoW and concentration camps were relieved of their sufferings. In its forays into Germany, the SAS was one of the first military units to reach a concentration camp at Bergen-Belsen.

Coming Home

Having been taken to the Villa Chagrin near Bayonne, in January 1943, Andrée de Jongh was transferred to the prison at St-Gilles in March 1943, where both her mother and sister Suzanne were being held.[1] Due to her involvement in helping Allied airmen to escape, Andrée was due to stand trial in Germany and arrangements were made for her to be transferred in the first instance to Essen, a large town in the Ruhr, where a tribunal would decide on her fate. She and many others were put on a train on 29 July 1943, which then travelled the 200km from Brussels to Essen. On arrival, they were marched to the prison, passing through a town ruined by Allied bombing. They spent most of that time locked up in their cells, given a sparse diet of bread, soup and ersatz coffee and allowed to take a twenty-minute walk each day.

After about fifteen days, they were put on a train to Zweibrücken on the West German border with France. Again, they marched to the prison, situated on the edge of a forest. The prison was infested with fleas and other pests. After about three weeks, Dédée came across her sister Suzanne. They were overjoyed to see each other and Suzanne informed Dédée that their mother had been moved to another prison within Brussels. At the end of September, they met Andrée Dumon, who brought them up to date with her own arrest and the arrest of her parents.

By January 1944, they were off to the station again and Dédée, Suzanne and Nadine managed to board the same carriage. The train headed north, towards Westphalia and Mesum. After about a month at the prison there, Dédée was taken back to Essen, separating her from her beloved sister. She stayed at Essen until 25 January, when she was put on a train that travelled in an unknown direction, stopping occasionally for air raid warnings before moving on under the cover of night. After three days and three nights, they arrived at Kreuzberg in Upper Silesia, near the Polish border, where there was a camp that accommodated Belgians among other nationalities. Here Dédée came across Jeanne d'Ursel, who had given birth while at the prison in Düsseldorf but who was now separated from her baby.

When spring arrived, the women were taken to work in the fields, where they managed to supplement their meagre diet with vegetables. They felt a surge of hope when someone informed them that the Allies had landed at Normandy. However, November 1944 arrived with no liberation in sight, and they were now faced with another journey. When the train finally stopped, the doors were flung open and they were met with a hail of abuse and shouting by SS guards, accompanied by barking and snarling dogs. They were forced ruthlessly into marching order and any who were slow to move were subjected to a beating. When they arrived at the gates of Ravensbrück concentration camp, the guards repeatedly counted them, a practice with which they would become all too familiar once they had entered the camp. They were taken to a vast tent, where they were met by a nauseous stench and a scene of abject suffering. Some of the cadaverous forms lying on the ground cried out to them for help. Dédée was dumbstruck with horror and she and her companions wondered if they would suffer the same fate. They then passed into a building, where Dédée was given the number 89970. It seemed an odd present to be given, for 30 November was her twenty-eighth birthday.

After a shower, they passed into another building, where they were told to leave all their clothing and possessions. They moved into a de-infestation area before being given ill-fitting clothing to cover their naked bodies. The next stop was their lodgings, or Block 32 in Dédée's case. Here bunks were crowded together, forcing inmates to climb over each other and compete for the best places. Dédée saw a skeletal apparition coming towards her that conjured up memories of someone she knew. Then she realised that it was her sister Suzanne. They fell into each other's arms. Dédée finally had the best of presents on her birthday. Suzanne guided Dédée over to meet others whom she knew from the past, including Elsie Maréchal, who told her that her father had been executed at the Tir National along with others and how Jean Greindl had been killed in an Allied bombing attack on the barracks where he was being held.

Dédée shared a mattress with her sister and, despite the appalling environment, managed to get some sleep, only to be woken by the awful wail of a siren at dawn and to join the rush for a scrap of food and drink and a turn at the overloaded latrines. Then they went outside into the freezing wind to stand in perfect lines as if they were new recruits at boot camp.

After being counted several times, some inmates were sent out to work on the land while others stayed in the camp to carry out a variety of tasks, including cooking or carrying coal. At all times, they were subject to the cruelty of their wardens and their female assistants, or *Aufseherinnen*, accompanied by aggressive dogs. The food was as ever insufficient to cover their nutritional needs and the level of physical effort they were forced to make each day. To make things worse, the climate at Ravensbrück was harsh and their clothing too light to maintain body warmth, leading to even greater loss of energy and debilitation. In order to boost the flames in the block stove, Dédée and Suzanne burned some of their bed boards, although this meant that they almost fell through their bed. They expected and received no pity from the heads of the block, or *Blockowa*, or their assistants, the *Stubowa*. The atmosphere was degrading and some inmates resorted to stealing. Dédée fought against this primitive urge for self-preservation and indifference to the suffering around her. The Nazis had set out to degrade them and the only way to defeat them was by maintaining their dignity, despite everything. Although she could not avoid the suffering, she could fight to avoid losing her soul.

Andrée de Jongh discussed these matters with a religiously minded friend, Cecile Hermey, who pointed her towards Christian teaching on the subject of suffering, including the passage from the Gospel of

St John about the grain of wheat. The grain that falls to the ground remains a single grain, whereas the one that dies produces fruit. It is not entirely clear how this should be interpreted in the circumstances of a concentration camp where they were all struggling to survive, despite the unrelenting efforts of their captors to destroy them. However, it may be seen to reflect an attitude of mind whereby the victim does not compromise with the enemy but gives themselves up in trust. Hermey also pointed to the Sermon on the Mount, including the passage, 'Blessed are those who weep for they shall be comforted.' To be called blessed amid abject suffering was another source of consolation. To what extent Dédée discovered her faith at this time is a matter of conjecture. What is clear is that this plucky young woman instinctively understood the message of embracing suffering while not surrendering to it.

On Christmas Eve, a Comet line helper who had been arrested along with her two daughters at the time of the Maréchal affair, Madame Davreux, died and both Dédée and Elsie Maréchal helped Madeleine Davreux take her mother to the incinerator. They had to leave her body on the pile of those awaiting incineration. As Christmas Day dawned, they heard a voice singing Christmas carols. The voice was that of a Canadian woman in the infirmary who died a few days later. Drawing on her experience and training as a nurse, Dédée did her best to alleviate the suffering of those who were enduring dysentery, typhoid and other diseases.

As they continued to plumb the depths of inhumanity, the Nazis sent the older women to a part of the camp ironically called the *Jugendlager*. Here they were subjected to accelerated discipline and longer parades by way of breaking their remaining strength. Jeanne d'Ursel offered to accompany the women in order to give them support. It was such acts of compassion and courage that instilled hope in others and opened the way to victory over inhumanity and hate. At the other end of the spectrum, the Nazis also had plans for the youngest among them. Several Polish girls had been used as guinea pigs for a variety of medical experiments and were visibly scarred as a result. As the Allies drew ever closer, the Nazi authorities were keen to get rid of the evidence of their barbaric practices and decided

to arrange for the execution of the girls. Before the plan could be
carried out, the women from the blocks managed to smuggle the
girls into areas where they knew the guards did not normally go and
thereby saved their lives.

On 1 March, the inmates were given short notice that they were
to leave. They only had a few minutes to get their meagre belongings
together before gathering for the parade outside. They marched to
the station, where they were made to wait before being loaded on
to cattle wagons. They had neither food nor water to sustain them,
though eventually one of the guards threw a block of snow into
their wagon. The train set off on a journey that lasted four days
and four nights, during which they were never allowed to leave the
wagon. Through gaps in the wagon boards, they could make out the
devastation caused by Allied bombing. When they finally arrived at
their destination in Austria, the wagons were emptied and several
dead bodies were thrown out. They were made to wait on the platform of a village called Mauthausen and when night fell they were
ordered to march towards the camp. One of the women fell over and
was immediately shot in the back of the neck.

The camp was situated at the top of a hill above the town and for
the women, weakened by their long journey and by lack of food and
water, the climb up the hill was a calvary. When they finally reached
the camp gate, they were made to wait outside in the freezing wind
and snow. When they were eventually allowed in, they were shocked
by the skeletal appearance of the men in the camp. As this was a
mainly male camp, their introductory routines of disinfection were
carried out by men. Soon after their arrival, the women were sent
out to work on a railway line that had been bombed by the Allies.
Several of the women were killed in another bombing attack and the
remainder decided to protest against the work. The protest attracted
the attention of the camp commandant, who told the women that
anyone who refused to work on the railway would be shot, starting
with the interpreter. At this point, Andrée de Jongh stepped forward
and told the commandant that the interpreter was speaking for all of
them. The commandant repeated his threat and Dédée replied that
in that case they would rather be shot. A guard struck her across the

face and Dédée and the interpreter were placed in solitary confinement, while the rest of the women, who had been told that Dédée and the interpreter would be shot if they did not co-operate, went off to work on the railway. Fortunately, there was no more bombing and in due course the Nazis concluded that emaciated women could not make much of an impression on railway cars and bent rails. When Dédée emerged from solitary confinement, she was struck by the solidarity that had been shown by the women, which in turn had been kindled by witnessing her own courage in speaking up and standing up for them all.

This incident demonstrated once again the special qualities of Andrée de Jongh and the philosophy of the Comet line as a whole, which was to fight without arms. Those who turn the other cheek, an often-misunderstood concept, do not give in; they stand their ground and are witness to the truth. It is not a sign of weakness but of strength. By speaking truth to power, in this case in the form of the camp commandant, Dédée was made to suffer in the short term but she was the moral victor. This was more than just endurance and survival; she renewed the courage and determination of all her fellow inmates.

A rumour started to circulate through the camp that the Red Cross were coming. In due course, they were marched into a square where they saw men dressed in civilian clothes, raising their hopes that help was at hand. They were not to be disappointed. Soon they were led out on to a plain outside the camp perimeter and made to stand in the cold. But this time the cold was tempered by the fires of hope. Then they heard the sound of an engine. It gradually grew louder and then a white vehicle appeared, covered in red crosses.[2] It was soon followed by others until there were fifteen vehicles on the plain. The men who got out of the vehicles started to speak to them in English and told them that they were to be taken to Switzerland. The women laughed and embraced with joy. The Red Cross workers told them that they would take the sick first and gradually the vehicles were filled and disappeared one by one. There was a growing sense of panic among those still waiting that they might be left behind and that they would have to return to the hell of the camp.

As the last vehicle left, they were indeed marched back into the camp but fortunately it did not prove to be for a long time. Soon they were marched out again to see the white vehicles awaiting them. This time, they did not miss the bus and soon they were on the way. They reached the Swiss border on 27 April in the afternoon. They got out to stretch their legs and were given chocolates and biscuits. Then they were driven to a station, and when the bus doors were opened, they were surprised to see nurses reaching out to help them get down from the vehicle. They had forgotten what it was like to be treated with humanity and compassion. They got on a train that took them to St Gallen, where they were sheltered in a school that had been emptied for the purpose. The school staff and children had left messages on all the blackboards: '*Wilkommen*'.

Apart from Dédée herself and her sister Suzanne, others associated with the Comet line who were also rescued included Andrée Dumon, Elsie Maréchal, mother, and Elsie, daughter, and Elvire Morelle.

Epilogue

Once Dédée de Jongh had been debriefed, she returned home to Brussels and in due course resumed her nursing studies. However, this was not before various Allied nations had given her some of the highest awards at their disposal. The British awarded her the George Medal, which she received from King George VI himself on 13 February 1946.[1] The United States awarded her the Medal of Freedom with Golden Palms.[2] France made her a Chevalier de la Légion D'honneur and her own country made her a Chevalier de l'Ordre de Léopold, the Croix de Guerre, or Oorlogskruis, and she was also given the honorary rank of lieutenant colonel in the Belgian Army. Years later, in 1985, she would also be made a countess by King Baudouin. The British Secretary of State for Air, Lord Stansgate, and Marshal of the RAF Lord Tedder awarded her a clock from a British bomber on behalf of RAF Bomber Command.

Although Dédée received all these awards with characteristic grace, one can imagine that her true reward was to have achieved what she set out to do: to enable Allied airmen to return to their bases in England where they could continue the fight for the liberation of occupied Europe.

As they had so much in common, it is not surprising that Dédée and Jean-François Nothomb should have become romantically involved. They were engaged to be married but it was not to be. Jean-François announced that he was going to Algeria to become a monk or Petit Frère de Jésus, following the teachings of Charles de

Foucould.[3] Although her heart must have been torn, Dédée was too big a person to let her emotional pain compromise her mission. With typical generosity, she recognised and celebrated the fact that Jean-François had found his vocation, and it appears to have given her greater clarity about her own vocation. Her work as a designer had not brought her fulfilment. She wanted to do something that would help others. When Jean-François departed for Algeria in September 1949, Dédée took up work in a tuberculosis sanatorium in Waterloo. This reinforced her conviction that her vocation was to mitigate the sufferings of others and she decided to resume her nursing studies. In September 1950 she returned to the nursing school of Saint-Camille. By June 1953, she had received a nursing diploma with distinctions from the Institut les Deux Alices. Her dream of helping lepers in Africa was soon to be realised. She enrolled in the Institut de Médecine Tropicale at Anvers and in July 1954 she received a certificate that enabled her to apply to serve as a nurse in the colonial services of the Belgian Congo.

Dédée worked in the Congo for six years, during which time she received a visit from the novelist Graham Greene, who was visiting the area in search of a character for his next novel.[4] Greene remembered that, despite the circumstances, de Jongh told him stories about her exploits during the war with a dash of humour. From the Congo, de Jongh then moved to Addis Ababa in Ethiopia, where she carried out the same kind of work in support of lepers for eleven years. When it became apparent that her mother was fading, RAF Transport Command re-routed a training flight from Aden to England via Addis Ababa so Dédée could visit her and did the same in reverse after her mother's funeral.

Despite her customary cheerfulness in the face of difficulties, Dédée's health had been permanently affected by her concentration camp experiences and therefore, while her life and activity was dedicated to helping others, she also needed support herself. She suffered from occasional epileptic fits, after which she went through a period of amnesia. Help was provided by her companion at the leper clinic Miss Thérèse de Wael.[5] Between the two of them, they provided care and hope for around 4,000 leprosy patients. After Addis Ababa, de Jongh then moved to Dakar in Senegal to carry out similar work.

Before she left Dakar, Dédée found out from a relation of Jean-François who worked in the Belgian diplomatic corps that he had left his monastic vocation and had married an Italian woman. They had a baby girl and were living in Rome. This news was soon confirmed in a letter from Jean-François himself.[6] It is easy to imagine the shock that Dédée must have experienced at this news. However, Dédée chose to admire Jean-François for his courage in making a difficult decision that would have attracted much criticism. In June 1981, she and her loyal nursing companion, Therese, left Dakar. After twenty-seven years of fighting leprosy and supporting those who suffered from this terrible disease, it was time to go home.

In August 2002, Dédée moved to the Institut National des Invalides de Guerre in Uccle. Thérèse joined her later and the two were able to spend time together, with Thérèse managing Dédée's diary of visitors. After her ninetieth birthday, Dédée's health declined rapidly and on 13 October 2007 she died at the hospital of Notre-Dame de la Cambre. She was buried next to her parents at Schaerbeek cemetery.[7]

The Pyrenees mountains are renowned for the beauty of their night skies. On a clear night, the whole galaxy seems to be on display. If you stayed for long enough, you might be lucky enough to see a comet. However, amid the innumerable stars, you can be sure to see one star that is brighter and stronger than all the others. This is the pole star – the sure and unwavering guide.

Principal Characters

Comet

Andrée de Jongh (Dédée): Comet founder member and leader. Awarded the George Medal and US Medal of Freedom with Golden Palms, Belgian Order of Léopold, made a Belgian Countess and French Chevalier de la Légion D'Honneur.

Frederick de Jongh (Paul): Father of Andrée de Jongh and Comet leader in Paris. Executed at Mont Valerien, Paris, 28 March 1944.

Suzanne Wittock, née de Jongh: Sister of Andrée de Jongh and Comet agent.

Arnold Deppé: Comet founder member. Arrested, sentenced to death but sentence commuted to being sent to a concentration camp.

Henri de Bliqui: Comet founder member.

Baron Jean Greindl (Nemo): Comet leader in Brussels, based in the Swedish Canteen. Killed during Allied bombing of Etterbeek Barracks, 7 September 1943.

Andrée Dumon (Nadine): Comet agent recruited by Frederick de Jongh. She was betrayed and arrested.

Michelle Dumon (Lily or Michou): One of the most experienced and successful Comet members. Awarded the George Medal and US Medal of Freedom.

Jean-François Nothomb (Franco): Comet leader in southern section.

Philippe d'Albert-Lake: Comet leader in Paris and married to Virginia.

Virginia d'Albert-Lake: Comet leader in Paris who was arrested and deported.

Elvire de Greef (Tante Go): Vital Comet link in southern France. Awarded the George Medal and US Medal of Freedom.

Charles Morelle: French officer and Comet agent. Arrested and died at Dachau concentration camp, 18 May 1945.

Elvire Morelle: Comet agent and sister of Charles.

Madeleine Bouteloupt: Comet helper betrayed by Jean Masson.

Robert Ayle: Comet leader in Paris. Executed by Nazis at Mont Valerien, 28 March 1944.

Germaine Ayle: Comet helper in Paris.

Yvon Michiels (Jean Serment): Comet leader in Belgium who succeeded Jean d'Ursel.

Henriette Hanotte (Monique): Comet line member. Escaped to England after having been compromised by a Belgian collaborator. Awarded MBE by the British.

Georges Maréchal: Belgian resistance member. Arrested and executed at the Tir National, 20 October 1943.

Elsie Maréchal (mother): Comet agent. Arrested and deported to Germany. Survived the concentration camps.

Elsie Maréchal (daughter): Comet agent. Arrested, violently interrogated and deported to Germany. Survived the concentration camps.

Peggy van Lier: Comet agent. Arrested but freed and escaped to England, where she married MI9 officer Jimmy Langley.

Victor Michiels (Louis): Comet agent who was shot while investigating the whereabouts of Elsie Maréchal.

Francia Usandizaga: Owner of the farmhouse in Urrugne that was the final stop before evaders and their guides set off over the Pyrenees. She was arrested along with Andrée de Jongh and died in a concentration camp after being beaten by a guard.

Florentino Goikoetxea: Indispensable Basque guide to the Pyrenees mountain routes that took many evaders to safety. Awarded the George Medal and Légion d'Honneur.

Traitors and Collaborators

Jacques Desoubrie, alias Jean Masson and Pierre Boulain: Significant Nazi collaborator whose activities led to the arrest of, among others, Frederick de Jongh and Jean-François Nothomb.

Prosper Dezitter: Regarded by the British as the most dangerous Nazi collaborator in occupied Europe, he organised parallel escape networks designed to deceive Allied evaders and lead them into the Nazi net. Dezitter moved to Germany where he was eventually arrested. He was sent back to Belgium where he was tried and sentenced to death.

British Intelligence

Michael Creswell (Monday): Diplomat and MI9 representative at the British Embassy in Madrid.

Airey Neave (Saturday): MI9 officer responsible for northern Europe.

Jimmy Langley: MI9 officer.

Arthur Dean: British vice-consul in Bilbao.

Donald Darling (Sunday): MI9 officer with an extensive knowledge of Spain and Portugal.

John Beevor: SOE agent in Lisbon who helped to organise resistance in case of a Nazi takeover.

Marathon

Albert Ancia (Daniel Mouton): Head of Operation Marathon in Belgium.

Jean de Blommaert (Rutland): Head of Operation Marathon in France.

Georges d'Oultremont: Comet leader who helped organise the Marathon operation and later joined the Belgian SAS.

Capitaine Dominique Edgar Potier: Belgian air force officer who helped organise Mission Martin in Belgium and the Possum line in France. He was captured by the Gestapo and died under torture.

Squadron Leader Lucien Boussa: One of the main organisers in the Fréteval camp.

Corporal Conrad Lafleur (Toussaint): French Canadian wireless operator.

Organisations

Abwehr: German intelligence service responsible for espionage, counter-intelligence and sabotage.

Geheime Feldpolizei (GFP): The secret field police of the German Wehrmacht.

Gestapo: Geheime Staatspolizei or secret state police, the political police of the Nazi state whose role was to eliminate all opposition to the Nazis. Its name is synonymous with Nazi brutality.

IS (9): Intelligence School 9, responsible for training military personnel in escape and evasion.

LOAC: Laws of Armed Conflict, also known as International Humanitarian Law, which governs the treatment of prisoners of war and other related matters.

Luc: Clandestine Belgian intelligence gathering service.

MI9: British Military Intelligence section 9, responsible for supporting military personnel in escape and evasion.

MIS-X: American equivalent to MI9, set up to help prisoners of war and escapers and evaders.

OSS: Office of Strategic Services, US equivalent of SOE.

RSHA: Reichssicherheitshauptamt or Reich Security Main Office, established by Heinrich Himmler and later headed by Reinhold Heydrich to fight enemies of the Reich both inside and outside Germany.

SD: Sicherheitsdienst, the SS intelligence service.

SERE: Survival, Evasion, Resistance and Escape.

SiPo: Sicherheitspolizei, the Nazi security police.

SIS: British Secret Intelligence Service.

SOE: Special Operations Executive, formed to create disruption in occupied Europe and to work with resistance organisations.

White Brigade: Belgian resistance organisation.

Zero: Belgian resistance organisation.

Chronology

1940

22–25 May: Battle of Boulogne.
22–26 May: Siege and fall of Calais.
27 May–4 June: Dunkirk evacuation.
12 June: Surrender of the 51st (Highland) Division at St-Valery-en-Caux.

1941

June: Arnold Deppé made first recce run down escape line to south of France.
15 July: Dédée and Deppé escorted ten Belgians to Spain.
August–September: Dédée escorted Sgt James Cromar and three Belgians via
    Valenciennes, Bayonne, Anglet and St-Jean-de-Luz before crossing the Pyrenees
    and going to the British Consulate in Bilbao.
November: Arnold Deppé sentenced to death, later commuted to concentration camp.
6 December: Dédée escorted Sergeant Jack Newton, Hilary Birk, Pilot Officer
    Howard Carroll and Belgian official Gerard Wauquez to Spain.

1942

6 February: Dédée accompanied Elvire Morelle over the Pyrenees with Englishman
    Jackie Hogan. Andrée Dumon joined the Comet team.
30 April: Frederick de Jongh left Brussels for the last time.
1 June: Dédée escorted three evaders, Robert Horsley, Lesley Baverstock and
    Canadian Harold de Manc, to Spain.
2 July: Dédée's sister, Suzanne, arrested by the Nazis.
19 November: Two German secret police disguised as American RAF pilots arrested
    members of the Maréchal family in Brussels. Peggy van Lier also arrested.
6 December: Peggy van Lier crossed the Pyrenees.

1943

January: Andrée de Jongh arrested by Germans.

29 January: Baron Selys de Longchamps attacked Gestapo HQ in Brussels in RAF Typhoon.

6 February: Baron Jean Greindl arrested.

March: Dédée transferred to the prison of St-Gilles.

29 April: Greindl condemned to death.

May: Count Antoine d'Ursel (Jaques Cartier) took over Comet operations in Brussels.

7 June: Frederick de Jongh, Robert Ayle, Germaine Ayle and several evaders arrested by Gestapo after betrayal by Jacques Desoubrie, alias Jean Masson.

29 July: Dédée sent to the prison at Essen in Germany.

7 September: Greindl killed during Allied air raid in Brussels.

28 September: Jean-François Nothomb (Franco) arrived in Spain to talk to Michael Creswell.

1 October: Start of Operation Ratweek by the Special Operations Executive (SOE).

20 October: Albert Maréchal and others executed at the Tir National in Brussels.

23–24 December: Antoine d'Ursel (Jacques Cartier) drowned in Bidassoa river.

29 December: Nothomb and Florentino escorted four more airmen over the Pyrenees and met Michael Creswell.

1944

January: Nothomb met Lily Dumon (Michou) in Elvire de Greef's house.

8 January: Nothomb and a companion arrived at the Gare du Nord in Paris.

10 January: Lily Dumon met Jacques Le Grelle (Jerome).

17 January: Le Grelle arrested by Gestapo at rue de Longchamps.

18 January: Nothomb arrested at rue de Longchamps.

28 February: Lily Dumon crossed the Pyrenees to Spain, where she met Michael Creswell.

9 March: De Blommaert (Rutland) and Lafleur returned to London.

28 March: Frederick de Jongh executed at Mont Valerien.

9–10 April: De Blommaert and Albert Ancia (Daniel Mouton) parachuted into France.

May: De Blommaert set up HQ near Fréteval Forest with help of Belgian RAF officer Lucien Boussa.

6 June, D-Day: Airey Neave landed at Arromanches and set up an HQ at Caen.

10 June: Virginia d'Albert-Lake arrested by Feldgendarmerie near Châteaudun.

11 August: Neave at Hotel Moderne in Le Mans, where he was joined by SAS Squadron under Captain Anthony Greville-Bell and by a unit of Belgian SAS.

14 August: Neave and Captain Coletta of MIS-X rescued 132 men from the Forêt de Fréteval.

15 August: Virginia D'Albert Lake deported to Germany.

1945

March: Dédée and her companions were transferred from Ravensbrück to Mauthausen concentration camp.

27 April: Dédée and her companions crossed the Swiss border to freedom, having been released from Mauthausen.

Notes

Introduction

1 *'Pour une fois que je disais la verité'*, *Les Femmes de l'Ombre*, Remi Kauffer. Kauffer describes the initial interrogation of Andrée de Jongh at St-Gilles prison, where the Germans ask for the name of the true leader of the Comet line. When she tells them that she is the leader, they do not believe her.
2 The plan was largely the brainchild of Field Marshal Alfred von Schlieffen, Chief of the German General Staff, 1891–1906.
3 General Helmuth von Moltke (the younger) was head of the German General Staff in the opening months of the First World War.
4 Diana Souhami, *Edith Cavell*, Quercus, 2010.
5 Ibid.
6 Ibid.
7 Ibid.
8 Catherine Butcher, *Edith Cavell: Faith before the Firing Squad*, Lion Hudson, Kindle Edition.
9 Souhami, op. cit.
10 Ibid.
11 Butcher, op. cit.
12 EC2 (16) IWM/Souhami op. cit.
13 'An Appeal to Truth: A letter addressed by Cardinal Mercier, archbishop of Malines, and the Bishops of Belgium, to the cardinals, archbishops and bishops of Germany, Bavaria and Austria-Hungary.'
14 Heinz Guderian had been much influenced by the ideas of Basil Liddell-Hart on tank warfare.
15 Lt Colonel E. Bauer, ed. Brigadier Peter Young, *The History of World War II*, Orbis Publishing, 2000.
16 C. in C. Portsmouth, 13.5.40, 51hd.co.uk.
17 Andrew Bradford, *Escape from Saint Valery-en-Caux: The Adventures of Captain B.C. Bradford*, The History Press, 2009.
18 Ibid.

19   Duke of Wellington's Regiment (West Riding) – Regimental Association,
     Pte Ron Boothroyd – WW2.
20   Martin W. Bowman, *RAF Escapers and Evaders in WWII*, Pen & Sword Aviation, 2014.
21   Ibid.
22   Ibid.
23   Ibid.
24   Ibid.
25   Ibid.
26   Ibid.

Chapter 1

1   Father Joseph André was a Jesuit curate at the parish of St Jean-Baptiste in
     Namur. Children were sheltered in the parish centre, with their persecutors
     as neighbours. They were then sent on to other religious foundations or
     families who could shelter them. Father André was a particular friend of the
     Jewish people and after the establishment of the state of Israel he was declared
     'Righteous Among the Nations'.
2   Hava Groisman was also known as Yvonne Jospa. She graduated from the Central
     School of Social Work in Brussels in 1933 and married Hertz Jospa the same
     year. They supported the Communist Party and the League Against Fascism and
     Anti-Semitism. She supported refugees from Germany, Austria and Spain. Hertz
     Jospa founded the Jewish Defense Committee in 1942.
         In 1964, Hava Groisman co-founded the Association of Jewish Former
     Resistance Fighters of Belgium.
         Hertz Jospa joined the Communist Party of Belgium in 1933. He was a
     member of the National Council of the Belgian League Against Fascism and
     Anti-Semitism. He was active in defending Jews from the summer of 1942
     onwards. He was arrested on 21 June 1943, imprisoned in Breendonk and then
     deported to several German concentration camps. Belgiumwwii.be/nl, Nico
     Wouters, Bruno de Never, trsl. Anna Asbury.
3   www.the-low-countries.com. Why the Belgium Resistance Deserves more Attention.
4   Secret Army: the Secret Army had about 54,000 members by June 1944.
     Belgiumwwii.be/nl op. cit. Belgium: A small yet significant resistance force
     during World War II, Kim de Vidts.
5   Bernard O'Connor, *Return to Belgium: The True Story of Four SOE Agents Sent in to
     Help Liberate Belgium during World War Two*, Bernard O'Connor, 2009.
6   Airey Neave, *Little Cyclone*, Biteback Publishing, repr. 2013, 2016.
7   Ibid.

Chapter 2

1   Rémy, *Réseau Comète*, Libraire Academique Perrin, Paris, 1966.
2   Neave, *Little Cyclone: The Girl who Started the Comet Line* (Dialogue Espionage
     Classics) (p.18). Biteback Publishing. Kindle Edition.
3   Rémy, op. cit.

4   Marie-Pierre d'Udekem d'Acoz, *Andrée de Jongh, une vie de resistente*, Editions
     Racine, 2016.
5   Ibid.

Chapter 3

1   For the full story of the capture and execution of Diana Rowden, Sonya
     Olschanezky, Andrée Borrel and Vera Leigh, see Rita Kramer, *Flames in the Field:
     The True Story of Four SOE Agents in Occupied France*, Michael Joseph, 1995.
2   From the Allied point of view, this was perhaps one of the most fortunate
     personality clashes of the Second World War. Senior German commanders
     such as Field Marshal Wilhelm Keitel and Hermann Göring thought that a
     German advance into the Iberian Peninsula should take priority over operations
     on the Eastern Front. They could see that taking Gibraltar would strangle
     British operations in the Mediterranean. The Iberian invasion, known as
     Operation Ferdinand and Isabella, was however shelved in favour of Operation
     Barbarossa, the invasion of Russia. In due course, the United States entered the
     war, Operation Torch, the Allied landings in North Africa, took place and the
     moment was lost. However, in the meantime, SOE kept its agents on standby
     in Gibraltar to encourage resistance activities in Spain should the Germans
     advance south.
3   Pere Ferrer, *Juan March, The Most Mysterious Man in the World*, Ediciones B, 2008.
4   Juan March was a Mallorcan businessman who had helped the British in the First
     World War by identifying the locations of German submarines in return for
     favourable terms for his smuggling operations. The head of British intelligence
     in Gibraltar is said to have called him 'my pirate'. In the Second World
     War, March was identified as a useful go-between when a plan was devised to
     bribe Spanish generals not to form too close a relationship with Germany. This
     arose from fears that Spain and Germany might combine in a land operation to
     invade Gibraltar. The plan was said to have been devised by British intelligence
     agent Alan Hilgarth and involved the deposit of $10 million in a US account to
     be used for bribes. Between $3 and $5 million were said to have been transferred
     to senior Spanish officials in 1942 alone. See Ferrer, op. cit.
5   John Beevor served in H-Section Special Operations Executive in Portugal,
     1941–42, under the cover of the post of Assistant Military Attaché. The
     diplomatic tension caused by John Beevor's activities was indicative of the
     tensions and complexities that underlay Britain's relations with Portugal at
     this time. Although Salazar himself and most of the Portuguese population
     were pro-British, Salazar did not think that the British could possibly win the
     war on their own. He was also a totalitarian leader whose dominance did not
     brook any opposition. At a time when the British, with good reason, feared a
     German incursion into the Iberian Peninsula, SOE was tasked with preparing for
     possible resistance activities, similar to those that were already taking place in
     occupied countries such as France and Belgium. This included plans to sabotage
     oil installations in the Tagus estuary as well as talks with potential resistance
     organisations. However, some of these resistance organisations were also opposed

to the Salazar regime and were monitored by the Portuguese International and State Defence Police (Policia Internacional de Defesa do Estado [PIDE]). Beevor claims that the Portuguese secret police had been trained in Berlin by the Gestapo and Sicherheitsdienst, and were largely pro-German. When one of Beevor's offices was used by a resistance activist who was later arrested by the secret police, Salazar was informed of the link with the British Assistant Military Attaché. (IWM 9482).

6   Survival Evasion Resistance Escape (SERE) Operations, Air Force Handbook 10-644, 27 March 2017.

7   The Hague Convention of 1899 included a 'Convention with respect to the Laws and Customs of War on Land' which 'forbids the killing of enemy combatants who have surrendered'. The treatment of prisoners of war during the Second World War was covered by the Geneva Convention on Prisoners of War of 27 July 1929. This was the basis of the Third Geneva Convention that was signed in 1949. The 1929 Convention did not replace the Hague Convention of 1899 but completed some of its provisions. The Convention on Prisoners of War (1929) was requested by the International Red Cross Conference after deficiencies were identified in the treatment of prisoners of war during the First World War.

8   aircforceescape.org.

9   Debriefing of Alan G. Johnston, Second Lieutenant, 722 Squadron, 305 Bomb Group, US National Archives Catalog (5554852), catalog.archives.gov/id/5554852.

10 Ibid.

Chapter 4

1   Rémy, *Réseau Comète*, op. cit.
2   Ibid.
3   Ibid.
4   RAF Commands, rafcommands.com.
5   Rémy, op. cit.
6   Geheime Feldpolizei, Author: Zurné Jan Julia (Institution: CegeSoma), www.belgiumwwii.be/belgique-en-guerre/articles/geheime-feldpolizei.html.

Chapter 5

1   Rémy, op. cit.
2   Ibid.
3   RAF Commands, rafcommands.com.
4   The crew of Halifax II W1219 who were taken prisoner were Flying Officer Denis Alban Thomas Churchward; Sergeant John Lamb; Sergeant Thomas Plumpton Milligan; Squadron Leader Clive King Saxelby and Sergeant R. Thompson.
5   Martin W. Bowman, *Escapers and Evaders of World War II*, Pen & Sword Aviation, 2014.

6   The casualties from Halifax W1188 were Sergeant Lawrence Fitsimmons (flight engineer), Squadron Leader Sidney Hoarce Fox (pilot), Sergeant Philip Charles Heath (air gunner), Flight Sergeant Norman Alexander Mercer (air gunner) and Sergeant Henry Frederick Wood (pilot). Two crew were made prisoners of war: Flight Sergeant Rowland Maddocks and Pilot Officer Geoffrey Wollerton.

7   Rémy, op. cit.

8   The RAF developed a variety of tactics to try to counter the Luftwaffe night fighter attacks, including the use of strips of aluminium foil or 'window' that were dropped at regular intervals by bombers. This created a blizzard effect on German radar screens and made it difficult for them to identify individual bombers. Bombers were also directed down corridors so that the effect would be to overwhelm the German early warning system and to prevent it from picking out individual bombers for attack. The RAF also took the fight to the enemy by deploying its own powerful twin-engine fighters, including the Bristol Beaufighter and the de Havilland Mosquito. These would lie in wait over Luftwaffe night fighter airfields and shoot down the night fighters as they took off. They would also follow them back to base after a raid. German night fighters included the Messerschmitt Bf 109G (2 × 30mm and 2 × 20mm cannon); Junkers Ju 88G6 (2 × 20mm cannon, 3 × 20mm cannon, 3 × 7.9mm cannon, 3 × 7.9mm machine guns); Dornier Do 217J (4 × 20mm cannon, 4 × 7.9mm machine guns, 1 × 13mm machine gun); and Heinkel He 219A (2 × 30mm machine guns, 2 × 20mm cannon, 2 × 30mm cannon).

9   Rémy, op. cit.

10   Ibid.

11   Ibid.

12   Ibid.

Chapter 6

1   Luc was founded in November 1940 by the Belgian Georges Leclercq in memory of his son Lucien, who had been killed in action in May 1940.

2   Royal Air Force Commands, details for Halifax W7750.

3   William Etherington, *A Quiet Woman's War: The Story of Elsie Bell*, Household Press, Norwich, 2002.

4   Ibid.

5   Ibid.

6   Ibid.

7   Ibid.

8   Ibid.

9   Neave, *Little Cyclone*.

Chapter 7

1   Rémy, op. cit.

2   Ibid.

3   Etherington, op. cit.
4   Ibid.

Chapter 8

1   Rémy, op. cit.
2   Ibid.
3   Ibid.

Chapter 9

1   Airey Neave, *Saturday at MI9*, Pen & Sword Military, repr. 2010.
2   No. 609 Squadron had previously flown Spitfires, and was credited as the first
     squadron to score 100 enemy kills. Once it had received the Hawker Typhoon,
     the squadron pioneered the use of the new aircraft in the ground-attack role for
     which it was so well suited.
3   Baron Raymond de Selys Longchamps had fought in the First World War, when he
     was awarded a British Military Cross. Apart from Jean, he had three other children,
     François, Monique and Ede. The two daughters were Belgian resistance fighters.
4   Neave, *Saturday at MI9*.
5   David Oliver, *Airborne Espionage*, The History Press, 2013 repr.
6   Ibid.
7   Neave, *Little Cyclone*.

Chapter 10

1   Neave, *Little Cyclone*.
2   Ibid.
3   Operation Catapult was a plan to prevent French naval vessels falling into
     German hands. The French fleet at Mers-el-Kébir was attacked by a British naval
     force, sinking one French battleship and damaging five others. More than 1,200
     French sailors were killed during the attack.
4   Neave, *Saturday at MI9*.
5   Reanne Hemingway-Douglass and Ron Douglass, *The Shelburne Escape Line*, Pen
     & Sword Aviation, 2015.
6   15th Fotilla MGB, Escape Lines Memorial Society and Spitfires of the Sea.

Chapter 11

1   Neave, *Little Cyclone*.
2   There is a memorial to Count Antoine d'Ursel, USAAF on the bank of the
     Bidassoa river. There are plans to erect a similar memorial for Second Lieutenant
     Jim Burch, USAAF.
3   Neave, *Little Cyclone*.
4   The Transportation Plan was designed to bring rail and other communications
     to a halt so that the Germans would be unable to send reinforcements to
     Normandy after the planned D-Day landings. It was developed by Professor

Solly Zuckerman, an adviser to the British Air Ministry, based on the broader plans of RAF Air Chief Marshal Arthur Tedder and the wider Overlord air plan, which had been drafted by RAF Air Chief Marshal Trafford Leigh-Mallory. The Transportation Plan would target bridges, rail centres, including marshalling yards and repair shops, rail lines and also German airfields in France and Belgium.

5   Neave, *Little Cyclone*.

Chapter 12

1   Developments in radar technology meant that by 1943 a map of the area beneath a bomber could be produced by radar. This was a combination of two technologies: the cavity magnetron, which distinguished objects on the ground from their radar signatures, and a scanning antenna and plan-position indicator. The system, known as H2S, became operational in early 1943 and was first deployed with the Pathfinder Force before being fitted to the rest of the bomber force. A similar system, known as ASV Mk III, was deployed by RAF Coastal Command to identify shipping.

2   KV-2-1732.
3   Ibid.
4   M.R.D. Foot and J.M. Langley, *MI9: Escape and Evasion*, The Bodley Head, 1979; repr. Biteback Publishing, 2020.
5   KV-2-1732.
6   Ibid.
7   Ibid.
8   Ibid.
9   RAF Commands, rafcommands.com.
10   Rafinfo.org.uk and W.R. Chorley, *RAF Bomber Command Losses of the Second World War 5: 1944*.
11   Ibid.

Chapter 13

1   RAF Commands, rafcommands.com.
2   Jean-Claude Galerne, *La Forêt de Fréteval, au couer du réseau Comète*, Les Editions Ella, 2014.
3   Rafcommands.com. The crew who died were Pilot Officer Henry French (pilot), Sergeant John Atkinson (flight engineer), Sergeant James William Randall (air gunner), Flying Officer Jack Stewart Thomson (air bomber) and Flying Officer Edmund Thomas Tinker (navigator).
4   Galerne, op. cit.
5   Second Lieutenant James F. Burch was shot down when co-pilot of a USAAF B-17F over Holland on 10 October 1943.
6   Maurice Petit, *Marathon en Ardenne: L'audacieuse mission de protection d'aviateurs alliés en 1944*, SNEL, 2022.
7   Galerne, op. cit.
8   Petit, op. cit.

9   Ibid.

10 Ibid.

11 Ibid.

12 USAAF Eighth Air Force Mission 300: 455 bombers and 766 fighters were despatched to bomb industrial targets at Schweinfurt, Zwickau, Oschersleben, Schkeuditz, Halle and Leipzig. However, the mission was called off due to the target being obscured by heavy cloud and haze. Six B-17s were lost and twenty-five B-24s were damaged.

13 Petit, op. cit.

14 Ibid.

Chapter 14

1   Virginia d'Albert-Lake, *An American Heroine in the French Resistance: The Diary and Memoir of Virginia d'Albert-Lake*, Fordham University Press, 2004.

Chapter 15

1   The Battle of the Scheldt was a costly campaign that, according to several senior commanders, including the British Admiral Cunningham, should have taken priority over other operations, such as the ill-fated Operation Market Garden. There was little point having a valuable port like Antwerp if Allied shipping could not approach it safely due to the presence of German forces in the Scheldt estuary.

2   The Ardennes Offensive, commonly known as the Battle of the Bulge, started with an offensive by the German Sixth Panzer Army on 16 November 1944.

3   The infamous Commando Order issued by Adolf Hitler on 18 October 1942 directed German forces to execute any British or Allied Commandos on sight, whether in uniform or not. It is said to have been in reaction to an incident on the island of Sark when British Commandos shot some German prisoners who were said to have been trying to escape. Whatever the cause, the Commando Order was in contravention of the Geneva Conventions, and this was confirmed at the Nuremberg Trials after the war.

4   Ben McIntyre, *SAS Rogue Heroes: The Authorized Wartime History*, Penguin, 2022.

5   Neave, *Saturday at MI9*.

6   Ibid.

7   Ibid.

8   Ibid.

9   Helen Fry, *MI9*, Yale University Press, 2020.

10 J.M. Langley, *Fight Another Day*, Pen & Sword Military, repr. 2013.

11 Ibid.

12 Cornelius Ryan, *A Bridge Too Far*, Hamish Hamilton, 1974.

Chapter 16

1   I am grateful to Marie-Pierre d'Udekem d'Acoz for allowing me to refer to the passage in her book about Andrée de Jongh, which covers Andrée's experiences in captivity, including both Ravensbrück and Mauthausen concentration camps. Marie-Pierre's research was based on lecture notes made by de Jongh herself.

2   The white buses that were sent out to the concentration camps were part of an effort largely instigated by the Norwegian diplomat Niels Christian Ditleff and the Swedish diplomat Count Bernadotte (1895–1948). Bernadotte negotiated with the Nazi authorities for the release of about 31,000 prisoners from the German concentration camps, having been appointed head of the Swedish Red Cross in 1943. He also negotiated prisoner exchanges that resulted in about 11,000 Allied prisoners being brought back to Sweden before being returned home.

The white bus operations took about two months and involved hundreds of Swedish and other medics and soldier volunteers. The transport and logistics support included thirty-six hospital buses, nineteen lorries, tow vehicles, field kitchens and fuel supplies for the return trip. Although a mission of mercy, the operation had to run the gauntlet of inadvertent friendly fire from Allied aircraft or bombing as the Allies continued their offensive against Nazi Germany.

Epilogue

1   WO 208/5452:
'Recommendation for George Medal
Mlle Andrée de Jongh
Recent History
Andrée de Jongh was twenty-five when, towards the middle of 1941, she started an escape line which in its long history has been responsible for the evacuation of more Allied service personnel than any other organisation. It was due to her and to her alone that the organised evacuation of Allied evaders and escapers took shape, and to this young girl of twenty-five falls the credit of having inaugurated a line which has brought freedom to so many evaders and enabled so many patriots to continue their work for the Allied cause. ...

From 1941 onwards until her arrest in January 1943 she continued to organise the despatch of evaders from Brussels to the Pyrenees. In all she was herself responsible for convoying 112 men in no less than 25 different parties. ...

For a year and a half she pursued her task tirelessly. Although both she and her father were pursued at an early date by the Gestapo, although arrest seemed daily imminent she refused to abandon her self-imposed mission. ...

Mlle de Jongh was arrested at the frontier on 13 Jan 43. From the prison at Bayonne she was taken to the prison at Fresnes. She was later transferred to Germany. After being sent to various prisons she was sent to the concentration camp at Mauthausen. Throughout the horrors of those two concentration camps her morale remained unbroken and at Mauthausen when women were ordered to work on removing debris on the railway lines (during which it was reported that over 50 were killed) she protested to the Germans on behalf of her fellow prisoners and was condemned to solitary confinement for three days. She returned to Belgium on 7th May 1945 via Switzerland greatly weakened by her experiences but with her morale unbroken.

Mlle de Nongh's career is one of outstanding gallantry and tenacious devotion to the Allied cause. It is a miracle that she did not pay for her devotion with her life. Both she and her family symbolise the very highest traditions of Belgian patriotism and courage.'

2   Citation of the United States, Medal of Freedom with Golden Palm:
'Andrée de Jongh, Belgian Civilian, for exceptionally meritorious achievements which aided the United States in the prosecution of the war against the enemy in Continental Europe, as a member of the Belgian underground movement, from August 1941 to January 1943. With extraordinary courage, ingenuity, and zeal she helped to conceive and operated the Comete Line, a thousand-mile escape route for Allied fliers falling in enemy occupied territory. In the face of almost insurmountable obstacles she personally conducted 118 Allied flyers to freedom, and more than four hundred airmen were returned to active duty through her genius for organization and her ability to inspire her co-workers. Though she was captured and imprisoned while convoying a group, she had so ingeniously designed her organization that it endured till the day of liberation. Her heroic self-sacrifice in the cause of freedom merits the highest esteem of the Allied Nations.'

3   Marie-Pierre d'Udekem d'Acoz, *Andrée de Jongh: Une vie de résistante*, Editions Racine, 2016.

4   Graham Greene, *In Search of a Character*, The Bodley Head, 1961.

5   d'Udekem d'Acoz, op. cit.

6   Ibid.

7   Ibid.

Bibliography

Beevor, Antony, *Ardennes 1944: Hitler's Last Gamble*, Penguin, 2016

Bishop, Patrick, *The Man Who Was Saturday*, William Collins, 2019

Bowman, Martin W., *RAF Escapers and Evaders in World War II*, Pen & Sword Aviation, 2014

Bowman, Martin W., *We Were Eagles: The Eighth Air Force at War, July 1942 to November 1943*, Amberley Publishing, 2014

Bradford, Andrew, *Escape from Saint Valery-en-Caux: The Adventures of Captain B.C. Bradford*, The History Press, 2009

Butcher, Catherine, *Edith Cavell: Faith Before the Firing Squad*, Monarch Books, 2015

Clutton-Brock, Oliver, *RAF Evaders: The Complete Story of RAF Escapes and Their Escape Lines, Western Europe, 1940–1945*, Grub Street, 2009

d'Udekem d'Acoz, Marie-Pierre, *Andrée de Jongh: Une vie de résistante*, Editions Racine, 2016

D'Albert-Lake, Virginia, *An American Heroine in the French Resistance: The Diary and Memoir of Virginia d'Albert-Lake*, ed. Barrett Litoff, Judy, Fordham University Press, 2006

D'Este, Carlo, *Decision in Normandy*, Penguin, 2001

De Vidts, Kim, *Belgium: A Small Yet Significant Resistance Force in World War II*, doctoral thesis, Hawaii, 2013

Eisner, Peter, *The Freedom Line: The Brave Men and Women who Rescued Allied Airmen from the Nazis During World War II*, Perennial/HarperCollins Publishers, 2004

Etherington, William, *A Quiet Woman's War: The Story of Elsie Bell*, Household Press, 2002

Evans, A.J., *The Escaping Club*, James McCann Company, 2015

Foot, M.R.D.; Langley, J.M., *MI9: Escape and Evasion*, The Bodley Head, 1979; repr. Biteback Publishing, 2020

Fry, Helen, *MI9: A History of the Secret Service for Escape and Evasion in World War Two*, Yale University Press, 2020

Galerne, Jean-Claude, *La Fôret de Fréteval, au Coeur du réseau Comète 1944*, Les éditions ELLA, 2014

Hastings, Max, *Bomber Command*, Pan, 2012

Hemingway-Douglass, Reanne; Douglass, Don, *The Shelburne Escape Line: Secret Rescues of Allied Aviators by the French Underground, The British Royal Navy and London's MI9*, Pen & Sword Aviation, 2015

Koreman, Megan, *The Escape Line: How the Ordinary Heroes of Dutch Paris Resisted the Nazi Occupation of Western Europe*, Oxford University Press, 2018

Kramer, Rita, *Flames in the Field: The True Story of Four SOE Agents in Occupied France*, Michael Joseph, 1995

Langley, J.M., *Fight Another Day*, Pen & Sword Military, repr. 2013

Levine, Joshua, *Forgotten Voices of Dunkirk*, Ebury Press in Association with the Imperial War Museum, 2010

Longden, Sean, *Dunkirk: The Men They Left Behind*, Constable & Robinson, 2008

Marnham, Patrick, *War in the Shadows: Resistance, Deception and Betrayal in Occupied France*, Oneworld, 2021

McIntyre, Ben, *SAS Rogue Heroes: The Authorized Wartime History*, Penguin, 2016

Neave, Airey, *Little Cyclone*, Biteback Publishing, repr. 2013, 2016

Neave, Airey, *Saturday at MI9: The Classic Account of the WW2 Allied Escape Organisation*, Pen & Sword Military, repr. 2010

Nicol, John; Rennell, Tony, *Home Run: Escape from Nazi Europe*, Viking Penguin, 2007

O'Connor, Bernard, *Return to Belgium: The True Story of Four SOE Agents Sent in to Help Liberate Belgium during World War Two*, Bernard O'Connor, 2009

Oliver, David, *Airborne Espionage: International Special Duties Operations in the World Wars*, The History Press, repr. 2013

Petit, Maurice, *Marathon en Ardenne: L'audacieuse mission de protection d'aviateurs alliés en 1944*, SNEL, 2022

Renault, Gibert 'Rémy', *Réseau Comète*, Libraire Academique Perrin, Paris, 1966

Ryan, Cornelius, *A Bridge Too Far*, Hamish Hamilton, 1974; repr. Hodder & Stoughton, 2015

Souhami, Diana, *Edith Cavell*, Quercus, 2010

Stourton, Edward, *Cruel Crossing: Escaping Hitler Across the Pyrenees*, Black Swan, 2014

Verranneman, Jean-Michel, *Belgium in the Second World War*, Pen & Sword, 2014

Websites

100thbg.com
158squadron.co.uk
384thbombgroup.com
51hd.co.uk
aafinfo.org.ukl
afhra.af.mil
aircrewremembered.com
aireyneavetrust.org.uk
airforcesescape.org

americanairmuseum.com
aviation-safety.net
baesystems.com/en-uk/heritage
belgians-remember-them.eu
belgiumwwii.be
coastal-forces.org.uk
cometline.org
conscript-heroes.com/escapelines
discovery.nationalarchives.gov.uk
eightyeighth.org
escape-and-evasionww2.com
europeremembers.com
evasioncomete.be
freebelgians.be
gthafhs.org
internationalbcc.co.uk
iwm.org.uk/collections
joint-forces.com
leprosyhistory.org
mi5.gov.uk
nam.ac.uk
nationalmuseum.af.mil
possumline.net
rafassociation.ca
rafcommands.com
rafmuseum.org.uk
redcross.org.uk
spitfiresofthesea.com
wartimememoriesproject.co.uk
wikipedia.org
ww2escapelines.co.uk
wwii-netherlands-escape-lines.com

Acknowledgements

I have drawn on several sources in this book to provide a tapestry of events surrounding the work of the Comet line. Although the narrative is written in my own words, I have relied on accounts which are based on first-hand interviews. These include the account by Gilbert Renault (Colonel Rémy), a notable resistance member himself, in *Réseau Comète*, and by other key players such as Airey Neave, who based his accounts in books such as *Little Cyclone* and *Saturday at MI9* on first-hand interviews and his personal involvement as a leading member of MI9. These are testimonies to events that cannot be found in any archive but which are essential to understanding how Comet worked and without which this book could not have been written. From the evaders' perspective, I have also drawn on accounts from various sources and from books such as *RAF Escapers and Evaders in World War II* by Martin W. Bowman. The workings of MI9 are drawn from Airey Neave's accounts and from books such as *MI9: A History of the Secret Service for Escape and Evasion* by Helen Fry and the previous history of MI9 by M.R.D. Foot and J.M.M. Langley, first published in 1979. My aim has been to draw on these various elements to create a picture of the Comet line in context of the various events that surrounded it. I strongly recommend that the reader should read these books and the others listed in the bibliography to benefit from the full story in their areas of expertise. I would also like to thank Marie-Pierre d'Udekem D'Acoz for allowing me to draw on her account of Dédée's experiences in

Nazi concentration camps in her book *Andrée de Jongh: Une vie de résistante* and for allowing me to use photographs from her collection. I have also drawn on much useful information from online sources including sites dedicated to the Comet line and to Air Forces Escape and Evasion Society (airforcesescape.org) as well as the excellent databases in RAF Commands (rafcommands.com). These and other resources are also listed in the bibliography. The correspondence pertaining to the identity and whereabouts of the traitor Prosper Dezitter and Operation Rat Week is drawn from the National Archives. The escape and evasion debriefing of 2nd Lieutenant Allan G. Johnston (USAF) comes from the US National Archives Catalog.

Finally, I would like to thank Amy Rigg, my commissioning editor at The History Press, for taking this project on in the first place and for her patience as the research and writing has evolved.

Index